The Cruise of the Widgeon. 700 miles in a ten-ton yawl. From Swanage to Hamburg, through the Dutch Canals, etc.

Charles Edmund Robinson

The BiblioLife Network

This project was made possible in part by the BiblioLife Network (BLN), a project aimed at addressing some of the huge challenges facing book preservationists around the world. The BLN includes libraries, library networks, archives, subject matter experts, online communities and library service providers. We believe every book ever published should be available as a high-quality print reproduction; printed on- demand anywhere in the world. This insures the ongoing accessibility of the content and helps generate sustainable revenue for the libraries and organizations that work to preserve these important materials.

The following book is in the "public domain" and represents an authentic reproduction of the text as printed by the original publisher. While we have attempted to accurately maintain the integrity of the original work, there are sometimes problems with the original book or micro-film from which the books were digitized. This can result in minor errors in reproduction. Possible imperfections include missing and blurred pages, poor pictures, markings and other reproduction issues beyond our control. Because this work is culturally important, we have made it available as part of our commitment to protecting, preserving, and promoting the world's literature.

GUIDE TO FOLD-OUTS, MAPS and OVERSIZED IMAGES

In an online database, page images do not need to conform to the size restrictions found in a printed book. When converting these images back into a printed bound book, the page sizes are standardized in ways that maintain the detail of the original. For large images, such as fold-out maps, the original page image is split into two or more pages.

Guidelines used to determine the split of oversize pages:

• Some images are split vertically; large images require vertical and horizontal splits.
• For horizontal splits, the content is split left to right.
• For vertical splits, the content is split from top to bottom.
• For both vertical and horizontal splits, the image is processed from top left to bottom right.

THE CRUISE OF THE WIDGEON.

THE "WIDGEON," YAWL, 10 TONS, IN SWANAGE BAY.

[*Frontispiece.*

THE

CRUISE OF THE WIDGEON.

700 MILES IN A TEN-TON YAWL.

FROM SWANAGE TO HAMBURG,
THROUGH THE DUTCH CANALS AND THE ZUYDER ZEE,
GERMAN OCEAN, AND RIVER ELBE.

BY

CHARLES E. ROBINSON, B.A.,

TRINITY COLLEGE, CAMBRIDGE.

With four Illustrations, drawn on Wood by the Author.

LONDON:
CHAPMAN AND HALL, 193, PICCADILLY.
1876.

LONDON:
BRADBURY, AGNEW, & CO., PRINTERS, WHITEFRIARS.

TO THE

FLAG-OFFICERS AND MEMBERS

OF THE

North-German and Isle of Purbeck Yacht Clubs.

CONTENTS.

———•———

CHAPTER I.

CHAPTER II.

CHAPTER III.

SWANAGE TO COWES AND ST. HELEN'S.

CHAPTER IV.

ST. HELEN'S TO SOUTHAMPTON.

CHAPTER V.

HAMBLE RIVER TO BOGNOR AND SHOREHAM.

CHAPTER VI.

SHOREHAM TO DOVER.

CHAPTER VII.

DOVER TO OSTEND.

CHAPTER VIII.

OSTEND TO BRUSSELS.

CHAPTER XVIII.

HARLINGEN TO LEEUWARDEN.

CHAPTER XIX.

LEEUWARDEN.

CHAPTER XX.

LEEUWARDEN TO DOKKUM AND THE LAUWER ZEE.

CHAPTER XXI.

OSTMAHORN AND THE LAUWER ZEE BY THE GERMAN OCEAN TO BRUNSBÜTTEL ON THE ELBE.

CHAPTER XXVII.

THE ELBE TO LONDON AND SWANAGE.

LIST OF ILLUSTRATIONS.

CRUISE OF THE WIDGEON.

CHAPTER I.

First idea of the Cruise—Cambridge to Poole and Swanage—The "Mate"—The "Windflower"—The "Dora"—Description of the "Widgeon" and "Waterbaby."

AFTER a pleasant summer spent in cruising on the Hampshire and Dorset coasts, and the land-locked Solent, the little yawl "Widgeon" folded her wings, and found a winter refuge, hauled up high and dry, at Poole. Meanwhile, the Widgeon's owner, one of the impatient tribe of yachtsmen, was full of schemes for the ensuing season, which, one after another, as schemes are wont to do, melted into thin air. So matters stood at the beginning of the Cambridge May term of 1874, when a random suggestion thrown out one morning at the breakfast table, fixed the direction of her wanderings.

The idea was, to start at the beginning of the "Long," sail up Channel to Ostend, and thence, making the best of my way to the Elbe, to visit my younger brother, at that time living in the family of the Haupt-Pastor of Brunsbüttel in Holstein, and finally to reach Hamburg.

This once resolved, never did May term seem to undergraduate so long, or Cambridge so uninteresting an abode. Still, some amusement was to be derived from the preparations for the cruise. A trustworthy skipper had to be engaged, various alterations effected in the Widgeon, charts and stores to be procured, and a tiny boat constructed under my supervision by "Robinson Crusoe," on his island in that part of the Cam popularly known as the "Freshman's river." Then, most important of all, some one had to be discovered who would share with me the pleasures and perils of the voyage. Luckily I found him at once, in the person of an intimate friend, whose nautical prowess, although he was more at home in the Third Trinity boat, will procure him in these pages the pseudonym of the "Mate." An engagement to row at Henley Regatta prevented his joining me, however, until the Widgeon put into Dover, about the end of June.

At last the time came to bid farewell for four long months to Cambridge, and away to London, whence in a few days more, I found myself rattling along the South-western Line, bound straight for quaint old fishy, sedentary Poole. Hardly fast enough to please me, we clatter through smoky metropolitan outskirts and mile upon mile of the green gladed Hampshire woods. Five minutes' unwilling halt at Basingstoke: one hasty glimpse of Winchester and stately old St. Cross: just a breath of the half-salt airs that flit about Southampton Water, and here stands old-fashioned, brick-built Poole, gleaming red in the afternoon sun. At last the hot wheels cease to roll, and the next moment I am hastening from the watergirt railway station, to the old shipyards whence many a famous clipper 'yacht has been launched in days gone by, my beacon a tall and stately topmast, I should know among a hundred. There lies my Widgeon, all a-taunto, white sails bent, snowy decks, and glistening sides—but, O Saunders! Saunders! did you not promise her for sea to-day, and here's your last wet coat of paint put on this very morning!

There's no help for it; she must sleep another night alone, and I must make my way to Swanage by the steamer "Heather Bell." The noisy whistle sounds, the paddles beat the water, the ceremony of turning the vessel round within her own length, is laboured through, and away we go down the smooth expanse of Poole Harbour. Steadily we range past Branksea Island, thick with trees, and past the old Crimean gunboat hauled up on the sandbank at Southhaven, doing duty as a dwelling for the coast-

guard.   Then over the shallows of Studland Bay and
through the sunlit ripple of tide off Handfast Point,
into the deep shadow of the hoary cliffs that stretch a
mile onwards to Ballard Head.   Next Swanage Bay
opens out before us, and the grand lines of downs that
guard the happy valley, disclose themselves, rank by
rank, until they vanish into the rugged horizon, from
whence the last of the giants, Creech Barrow, rears a
dark and solitary crest.

Now, with slow-moving paddles, we glide past the
stern of a large and handsome yacht, her tall spars
clearly reflected in the still water, where she sits
alone like a dreaming bird.   It is the "Windflower,"
bound with the next tide for Falmouth, and thence
away on a long summer cruise about Norwegian shores.

On the pier, as we sweep alongside, I meet her
owner, a college friend of mine, and after getting rid
of my portmanteau, am soon landed with him on the
deck of the new yacht.   The tide, which waits for no
man, will ebb ere two hours are gone by, so after a
dinner which does the genius of the galley great
credit, sundry noises above announce that the crew
are shortening scope of cable and manning peak and
main halliards, eager to be off.   In five minutes the
gig has borne me ashore ; quickly it regains the yacht's
side ; yo-heave-ho! with a will, and up comes the
anchor, out flies the jib, she slowly feels it, now she

moves under command   Let fly the weather jib-sheet and stand by the lee !—and away she glides out of sight westward round Peveril Point.

Light enough still remains to visit other friends and to board the schooner " Dora," new to me, which is to accompany her sister Widgeon during the first days of the cruise abroad.

And now, before entering on another chapter, I may as well briefly describe the little Widgeon and the tinier "Waterbaby," which came into being only to attend upon her.

The Widgeon was yawl-rigged, in every respect like a large yacht, and with her tall spars and bold sheer, had a handsome appearance on the water. Although not new, she had been so completely refitted in 1872, as to retain little of her old materials ; hull and gear were all sound and good, and her sails a well-cut suit. She measured something under ten tons, builders' measurement ; and the following were some of her principal dimensions :—

	ft.	in.
Length over all	34	7
Extreme breadth	8	10
Draught amidships	5	4
Deck to topmast truck	40	0
Mainmast, deck to hounds	20	10
Bowsprit, outboard	15	4

Of course, before embarking on so extended a

voyage, everything was attended to which was necessary for the comfort and safety of her crew. She was entirely stripped, recaulked, and repainted, in Saunders' yard at Poole, where she had been hauled up for the winter. A new lead keel, of thirteen hundred-weight, gave additional power of carrying sail, and at the same time lightened her, by allowing a greater quantity of iron ballast, which has less specific gravity, to be taken out.

The cooking stove, which burned coke, was discarded, and with it all the heat, dirt, disappointment and discomfort which formerly attended the preparation of every meal. In its place came on board two spirit lamps, of French invention, burning methylated spirit, without smell or danger, and twice as cleanly and effective. The cabin roof, which had not been quite watertight, was covered with thick painted canvas, tightly strained over it, so as to be at once neat in appearance and perfectly proof against the heaviest rain or spray. Tin plates and other utensils were substituted for crockery, which is too heavy and too liable to break, for use in a little yacht at sea. A new sheet anchor, a good aneroid barometer, a cabin clock, charts of the coasts we designed to visit, thick rugs for sleeping purposes, books of sailing directions, and countless other little necessaries, were procured and assigned to their proper places on board, where two new lockers were fitted to accommodate some of them. All the old rigging was replaced with new, and a trysail supplied by a sailmaker of Poole for use in possible gales.

Now let us go below, and see how every inch of space is utilized for one purpose or another. First comes the main cabin, about eight feet square, and four feet eight inches in height, just enough to enable us to sit down in comfort, without touching the ceiling with our heads. On either side is a berth, a trifle over six feet long, with lockers underneath it which contain the bedding. Cushions covered with green leather, serve as seats by day and mattresses by night. Light is admitted by four windows, two on either side, and there is besides a deck-light and a sliding hatch. In the middle stands a mahogany table, with two flaps, and a deep box under it serves as a locker for about thirty pounds of sea-biscuit, reserved for emergencies. At the fore end of the cabin hangs against the wall the swinging candle-lamp, and on one side is a door, which leads into the forecastle, through the pantry. Above the owner's head, in his berth on the starboard side, hang the aneroid barometer, the clock and a mercurial thermometer : books, charts, and other appurtenances are out of sight in drawers at the afterpart of the cabin, on either side of the brass-bound folding doors which lead into the cockpit. The latter is an open space aft, with its floor well down in the body of the vessel, so that the shoulders of people standing in it are on a level with the deck. The mainboom swings overhead, and the tiller and many important ropes can be worked from hence. There are lockers all round the cockpit, which serve as seats, under two of which lurk watertanks of zinc, which contain a supply of water, at a pinch, for four persons for a fortnight. Right aft, under the tiller, is the sail-room, which contains all our changes of canvas wings, and a few spare ropes and blocks.

Now going forward again, through the tiny pantry, with its shelves hung with pots and pans, we enter the forecastle, which is, of course, triangular in shape, and is about seven feet long and nearly as wide at the after end. There are lockers all round this too; side and riding-lamps are hung from its beams, and a mop and pail and a few tools lie about. A prism of thick glass, let into the deck, lights it up by day, when the hatch is closed in blowy weather, by a kind of tourniquet. Without this precaution the yacht would soon be in difficulties, for she is fond of going head and shoulders into the seas, when they meet her sharp bows in quick succession. I got a regular ducking one day, on going below to fasten the hatch, as we suddenly sailed out of smooth water to a spot where the tide was raising high short waves, by running against the wind.

The forecastle is too short and low to admit a swinging hammock, so a bed has to be constructed on the floor, and stowed away in the daytime.

Lastly, the tiny dinghy, the "Waterbaby," now claims a few words of notice. She is a very small boat, ten feet long and four feet broad. I had two little craft of this description already, but one unluckily was too small (only eight feet long) for this cruise, while the other, although a fine boat, was as much too large. The problem to be solved was to build a boat not more than ten feet long, which is the utmost length the Widgeon can stow on deck in bad weather, yet capable of carrying four persons safely in case of disaster; light and easy to row, and yet of sufficient stability to carry a small sail. These conditions I endeavoured to meet by designing the Waterbaby with a sharp but flaring bow, a round, easy bilge, flat bottom and gentle run. The main breadth occurs at about four feet from the stern, and is carried well aft, diminishing with a bold sweep towards the bows. She has a sheer of three inches, but as her sharp bow is decked over for three feet from the stem, a coaming was so arranged as to add three inches to the freeboard amidships, while its upper edge, being on the same level with the stem

and sternposts, the boat, when turned bottom upwards on deck, bears along the whole of the coaming,
the transom and the stemhead, and requires no
chocks to keep it from swaying to and fro.   There is
a little deck also aft, and the spaces between the
gunwale and the coaming of the cockpit (which is six
feet long, and has the form of a boat) are decked
over, except amidships, where the coaming stands
upon the gunwale.   The Waterbaby is constructed
of oak ribs, stem and stern, white pine planking and
red pine decks, and the covering strake is mahogany.
As for her performances they are chronicled further
on ; suffice it here to say, that although she might
be improved, yet on the whole she answered well.

CHAPTER II.

FRIDAY, the twelfth of June, was the beginning of a whole week of troubles; nevertheless the morning broke delusively fine, with a nice little breeze from N. E. I shipped in the Dora for Poole, and there found the Widgeon's paint still wet, especially the thick white priming on the new canvas-covered cabin roof, a most important provision if any comfort is expected in a small yacht at sea. None but the unfortunates who have tried it can imagine the pleasure of going to rest, on a rough, rainy night, in your narrow berth, when the yacht is pitching bows under, slapping her counter down on the waves as they roll away astern, and straining at her cable as the gusts of wind rush whistling through the rigging, while all the time, from a thin unprotected roof, warped by the sun and wind, a continuous drip, drip, drip is allowed to fall upon your face and over all the dry clothes that lie about.

It was late in the afternoon when my skipper,

Hescroff, a Poole man, came on board with his kit, and we set sail in pursuit of the Dora, which had started half an hour earlier. The wind had fallen light, and gone round to E., which gave us a dead beat down the harbour's narrow channel. We handed the jib and foresheets as if we were racing for a cup, and stiff as a church under her larger sails, the Widgeon began to gain upon the schooner hand over hand. In fact, as we rushed past the bell-buoy, in a little gust of wind, we could catch a glimpse of her mainpeak gliding along over the sand-hills at Southhaven, little more than half-a-mile ahead. Now came our first adventure.

Exactly opposite Branksea Castle there runs out from the mainland a tongue-shaped sandspit, stretching with a gradual shelve some forty yards under water, which is perpetually picking up vessels that are strangers to the locality. At high tide there is a depth of about six feet upon its extreme end, where it dips very suddenly into the deep channel, but on the ebb the greater portion dries, and the rest is all awash. Now both Hescroff and I knew exactly where this hidden trap lies in wait. Scores of times had we given it a wide berth, and scores of times crossed it in smaller boats, and we both knew perfectly well that, even at the very top of the flood, the Widgeon could not sail over. But there was the Dora bowling away a long half mile in front, and if we were to shave round the spit as closely as possible, one tack at least between the Havens might be saved, and a march stolen upon her. And thus we succeeded admirably in accomplishing the very thing we most wanted to avoid. Suddenly an ominous grating sound arose from under the keel, the bows slid upwards a few inches, and there we were hard and fast in the sand, within three yards of deep water!

Now this would have been annoying under any circumstances, but was particularly so now, because, expecting to be at Swanage before dark, we had put neither bedding nor provisions on board, nothing to drink, nothing to smoke, and no fuel. To add to our perplexities, there was nothing in the shape of a spare spar, with which to prop the yacht upright when the ebb tide made away. The evening sky looked dirty, and although our situation was protected from any sea, there still remained the uncertainty whether, when lying on her bilge, the yacht would right herself without filling. The Dora, guessing the nature of our mishap, held on to report it at Swanage, and we should have spent a miserable night indeed, had it not been for a fisherman who chanced to bear down upon us in his boat. While he was gone to fetch provisions from Poole, we extemporised supports out of two short spars procured from a pilot at Branksea, and then there was nothing left but to try and be as jolly as possible under the circumstances.

At about eleven o'clock, when the spirit of our imitation of Mark Tapley had already begun to droop, the fisherman re-appeared out of the darkness, and handed up a large hamper of cold provisions, pipes, tobacco, candles, and brandy. Directing him to return early next morning to our aid, after the heartiest of suppers, we turned in, with great efforts to go to sleep. Despite the cold, sleep came at last, and it must have been two o'clock in the morning when I was awakened by a sudden crash outside, a noise of the hamper and everything else moveable rolling and bumping across the cabin floor, combined with an unpleasant sensation of lying on my back, wedged in an angular trough! Rising and striking a match, I found myself standing on the lockers, the whole cabin lying at an angle of forty-five degrees with the totally invisible horizon, and every single article that had been stowed upon the starboard side tumbled in a confused heap about my legs. Only one object besides myself remained upright, and that was the swinging lamp, which took unfair advantage of the opportunity to smoke and crack its glass globe.

Looking out of doors, I found that the Widgeon was lying on her side, in scarcely six inches of water.

The strong squall of wind which had heeled her over
had forced the extemporised prop two feet into the
sand, so that it could not be pulled out. All around
was dark as pitch, and evidently nothing could be done
till morning; so into the cabin I turned again, with
the whistling wind and grinding surf on the bar outside in my ears, to lie down, but not to sleep.

Dawn appeared in the misty east while we were
yet lying on the tongue of yellow sand, completely
deserted by the water. Presently the sun rose, and
the flood came along, when to our great relief the
Widgeon began to float long before the wavelets
approached her open cockpit, so that we never afterwards had any fears on that score, in all the foreign
harbours and blind banks where we were subse-
quently fated to lie helpless from tide to tide. True
to his time, our fisherman came from Poole, and from
six till eight o'clock, when the flood was high, worked
with us incessantly at lightening the yacht, in the
vain hope of getting her off. Taking out nearly a
ton of iron ballast, we laid it in the fishing boat,
which was lashed to the end of the main boom
secured on the starboard side, giving a considerable
list in that direction, and a consequent additional
decrease in draught of water. Then setting mainsail,
jib and foresail to the light airs, and carrying the
sheet anchor out on the starboard bow, we manned

the windlass with a will, until the cable came taut as a fiddlestring under the great strain. All this labour, however, was to little purpose, for the tide did not rise so high by several inches as on the previous evening, and besides, the speed at which we had gone ashore had run the keel a long way into the sand. We were just about to give up in despair, when a tug steamer came by with a large vessel in tow, and the waves thrown up by her paddles successively floating the Widgeon, and then bumping her down on the bottom, we contrived, by heaving on the cable at the right moment, to gain about a couple of yards, only to stick fast again on the very edge of the spit. The ebb had already begun to make, and we replaced the ballast, compelled to wait for the evening tide, which was expected to be very high.

In the meantime I walked over the heaths to Swanage, and collected a pile of rugs and provisions, with which to revisit the Widgeon, on board of the never-failing Dora. Then came a pleasant sail to Poole, in the course of which we passed Hescroff busily employed in digging away the sand from the keel of my stranded ship. On our return we found her afloat, and after shipping the stores and restowing the ballast, both yachts had a spirited cruise to Swanage, in a fine slashing breeze, and the Dora took up her moorings in the bay. Ours, unluckily, were not yet laid down, and as the weather at nightfall appeared rather threatening, we resolved to return to the comparative quiet of Poole Harbour.

There the easterly wind kept the Widgeon imprisoned four tedious days, the monotony of which was only broken by the loss of an anchor off Branksea, and the occupation of arranging in their proper places all the cushions, lamps, plates, books, deck-seats, mops and brooms, ropes and spare blocks, tools, and the other innumerable fittings that make so much weight and so little show, aboard a small yacht. By Wednesday, the 17th of June, the Widgeon was in complete order, alow and aloft, and, tired of remaining in harbour, I determined, wind or no wind, to sail to Swanage next morning.

Accordingly, about noon we started in a northerly breeze, so strong as to make it all we could do to carry a double-reefed mainsail in the smooth water. However little or no wind was found in Studland Bay outside, and, shaking out both reefs, a delightful run with a light air over the perfectly calm sea, brought us to our destination early in the afternoon.

Only three days now remained, until the date which had been fixed upon for the commencement of our projected cruise. However, the forced stay in Poole Harbour had given so much opportunity for overhauling all our gear and stores, from truck to keel, that we could well spare Friday for a sail to Bournemouth in company with the Dora. It was one of those delightful mornings which form the real attractions of yachting, far more than days of double-reef breezes and copious drenchings of salt water, which some people say they like, but may generally be observed to avoid. A light and steady breeze just rippled the sunlit sea, while the sky, though clear and cloudless, was not of that intense and blinding blue that accompanies extreme heat.

On reaching Bournemouth we hove-to off the pier, and the Waterbaby had her first trial at sea with four persons on board. Of course the little thing was hard to pull, with her full stern deep in the water, and dragging after her a great backwash, but she was evidently safe enough and as stiff as an island.

It was evening when we returned to our moorings, which had been laid down on the previous day. Saturday passed quickly over in getting on board a supply of water for our tanks, and a whole cargo of biscuit, preserved meats, wine and other provisions; but Sunday was of course a *dies non.*

There is a story, by the way, of two fishermen at Swanage, who put off in their boat one Sunday morning, to haul a trot line set overnight. They had succeeded in bringing to the surface by might and main an enormous conger eel, whose gruesome countenance had just emerged from the water underneath their noses, when the creature, writhing on the hook, lifted its tail over the gunwale behind them, and brought it down with a thump on their bent backs! The shock was too much for their consciences, already burdened with a feeling of wrongdoing. They dropped their prize in panic terror, rowed home without stopping to look back, and lived ever afterwards in the firm belief that they had hooked a certain nameless personage, who is generally supposed to dwell in a rather warmer place than the bottom of the British Channel.

CHAPTER III.

SWANAGE TO COWES AND ST. HELEN'S.

The cruise begun—An old curiosity—Yachts in the Medina—Chasse-marée ashore—Bembridge and Sea View—Trials of the Water-baby—Pleasures of a "quiet" anchorage.—Yachting.

THE morning of Monday, the 22nd of June, with a clear sky and light south-westerly wind, broke most auspiciously for the intended cruise. Warm sunshine gleamed on the rugged grey stone houses of Swanage, the tops of the tall elms that grow close to the waterside, and the broad expanse of the semicircular bay, hedged round with huge cliffs. From an early hour the mainsail of the Dora had been quivering aloft, and shortly after ten o'clock, while we were yet unready to start, she swung round on her heel, and laid her course by compass for the Isle of Wight, still entirely hidden in the morning haze. Presently the Widgeon's mainsail and gaff-topsail too, rose by her crew's united efforts, and the large jib, deftly stopped along itself with half-cut yarns, was hoisted ready to burst into flowing folds at a moment's notice. A little crowd was collected at the pier head to bid us good speed, and they had a hearty laugh at the expense of our seamanship, when the Waterbaby by some misadventure went silently adrift, and had to be ignominiously towed back by a fisherman, who paddled after her in his dinghy.

At last about eleven o'clock I went to the helm, and, slipping from her moorings, the Widgeon flew off in pursuit of the Dora, now a mere speck in the distance. Running before the wind at the rate of about seven miles an hour, with the advantage of a large topsail, we were rapidly overtaking her, and the white cliffs of Swanage, were as quickly fading into indistinctness astern. It was delightful to lean upon the tiller carelessly steering, while the soft, warm air, the green unruffled sea, flecked with sparkling bubbles in our wake, and the clear blue sky, cooled rather than dimmed by an all-pervading mist, lulled every sense into calm, half-conscious enjoyment.

Suddenly my meditations were cut short by Hescroff, whose head is a perfect dictionary of all craft that sail in or out of Poole, pointing to an old coaster brig in the act of luffing across our bows.

"Keep her as she goes, sir; that brig will be through our lee and out on the weather-bow in another five minutes. That vessel," he went on to say, "is nearly a hundred years old, and there isn't hardly a port in the world where she hasn't landed a cargo in her time, and she's a good vessel still. She'd be a small fortune to a poor man."

"But do you really mean she's as old as that?" said I.

"Yes, sir, she is; but she's been well kept up, and there's precious little of the old stuff in her. She belonged to an old lady who never would have a vessel broke up if she was a lucky one like this here, not even to build another on the very same lines. I'd rather go skipper of her than many a brand-new craft. She'll carry four hundred ton easy, and bowl along, too, with it all."

While we were speaking the aged curiosity had slipped ahead, and altered her course to the southward of the Isle of Wight, of which we now caught our first glimpse.

Off Christchurch Harbour the mist began to clear from the horizon, and in another hour we were almost becalmed under the lee of the particoloured cliffs in Alum Bay, while a cutter yacht which had been sailing along-shore from Bournemouth, beam and beam with ourselves, was tearing away to leeward, under the guns of Hurst Castle, with a fine breeze in her sails. Yarmouth, with its quaint old tower and red-roofed houses backed by dark green trees, was passed before we got the wind again, but then it rushed with a will across the lower land about Newtown river, and hauling in sheets to meet the change in its direction, we began to march along very fast in the smooth water of the Solent. Soon the tall yellow masts of a fleet of yachts, lying at their moorings, made their appearance from behind the green rise of Egypt Point, and threading her way in and out among them, quite close to the villa-studded shore of West Cowes, the Widgeon rounded to her anchor in the Medina river, five minutes after the Dora, not long past three o'clock in the afternoon.

When all the sails had been neatly stowed, and protected by their painted canvas covers from dirt or wet, in a way to satisfy even the fastidious critics of the yachting metropolis, the crews of both yachts launched their dinghies and proceeded ashore, to market for fresh provisions and stores of every kind. Then, in the cool evening, came a row up the little Medina, between and among yachts of every form, size, and degree, from the splendid schooner "Shamrock" of two hundred and ninety-seven tons, whose immense clean spars tower full eighty feet into the air, to the tiny cutter of five tons measurement, whose mainmast one could almost break across the knee, both alike finished to such a pitch of workmanship as would make them fitting ornaments for some Brobdingnagian duck-pond.

On either side, the river mouth is thickly lined with busy ship-yards, where the clang of hammering iron is heard from morning to night, and higher up, where the Medina narrows in the country, more than a hundred yachts were lying securely berthed, their keels having worked themselves docks in the yielding mud. Not one of them showed any sign of life, but all lay stripped of sails and rigging, only the bare masts appearing above the deserted hulls. Another month and all would be on the wing, keeping one another's company in immense flights from regatta to regatta: but this was the dead season.

By the time we had passed in review all the denizens of the Medina, the sun had begun to set, and our boats wended their way back to the yachts at the river's mouth. Supper followed, on board the Dora, after which one of her cabin passengers came off and took possession of the port sofa-berth in the Widgeon, for the night.

It is not so very easy, until you get accustomed to such limitations as want of space imposes on two people trying to dress at once, inside a small yacht's cabin, to keep such early hours as need and custom require of those who go down into the sea in ships. Even if you rise betimes, and shiver through your early bathe with comparative, only comparative comfort, it requires a certain amount of endurance to go into every detail of your toilette without giving up in despair and breakfasting in the middle of it. Nevertheless, we being in a very correct latitude, and perfectly smooth water, made shift to pull on shoes and socks without knocking our heads against the cabin roof, to shave without upsetting the hot water, and then turn hungrily to a breakfast of luxurious pork chops, by say ten o'clock in the forenoon of Tuesday. Meanwhile the Dora's people, no idlers they, had got under way, and were disappearing behind Old Castle Point. Half an hour afterwards we were off in chase, and reaching lazily along with a light air in our lofty canvas, made her out very soon, among the sombre-looking quarantine hulks, off the muddy foreshore of Ryde. Passing close to the pier, the outstretched arm of that lively little town, we skirted the sand rather too closely, and only just hauled off in time, when a big French chasse-marée grounded under our very noses : fortunately for us, who were on the point of setting the example ourselves. What a noise her motley crew made, instead of setting quietly to work to get her off. As if they had not five or six hours' leisure for conversation in store, the tide being only about half-ebb !

Presently loomed in sight one of the great circular forts, bristling with guns from every point of the compass, and looking like a great iron vent for the ill-humours of the earth under the sea. Here we began to overtake our consort in tacking against the wind, and about midday both craft anchored within five minutes of each other, a mile off shore, in St. Helen's Road. After lunch every one but the two skippers landed in the Dora's boat at Bembridge, which place, like Constantinople, has a striking appearance from the sea, and on a closer inspection, is, at all events, much cleaner, if less important, than the Turkish capital. We roamed up the treeclad hill among quiet cottages with occasional pleasant glimpses of the Solent glittering far below, and then crossing Brading Harbour, disembarked at St. Helen's, the second volume in the series of which Bembridge and Sea View are the first and third. The same description will do for all three; since "each of them," as a mother of twins once wrote about her children, "not unfrequently appears more like its brother than itself!"

St. Helen's can point with pride to a little general shop, where we laid in such a stock of lucifer matches as rendered us personages of some consideration in the eyes of the old dame who sold them. I suspect her market was dull indeed.

Evening was closing in as we rowed back to the Widgeon, on board of which the Dora's people had been invited to an elaborate supper, and we turned in about ten o'clock. "Sky overcast, wind fresh, water smooth," says my log.

In yachting, as in everything else, the least agreeable of all states is forced inaction, the torturing spirit of calms and contrary winds, whose acquaintance we made on Wednesday morning. A disturbed night brought on a fresh breeze, almost half a gale of wind from S.W., which would have been awkward for us, had we not been lying under the lee of the Isle of Wight. Thick clouds pouring incessantly in hard fleecy masses of grey, from the windward quarter, gave no expectation of any approaching change of weather, so we had to resign ourselves to our fate, and spin out the time with writing up the log, smoking, and rowing trials of speed between the Waterbaby and the Dora's boat. Lurching and pitching about in the short white crested waves, the two little cockleshells were evenly matched, but the Waterbaby's foredeck threw off a good deal of the thick spray which dashed over her, wetting me handsomely as it flew.

In the afternoon, the wind having moderated, we all pulled off in the boats, and beaching them at St. Helen's, walked along the seawall under a plantation to Sea View, for provisions and fresh water, of which the "squadron" had run short. Returning at sunset, we spent a pleasant evening on board, and retired early to rest, with the sound in our ears of a strong wind moaning and groaning about the rigging. Now there is a lull, all is quiet for five minutes, then frap! —a pause, and again, frip! frap! frip! frap! the halliards rattle away on the mast, and we turn out half-dressed to lash them tightly round and round, but scarcely get warm again in bed, when with a crash and a bump the "baby" runs into us like an ironclad, making a woful dint in the glistening paint of our quarter. Out again in the drizzle to secure her bottom upwards on deck, and after this perhaps we may rest undisturbed, except when from time to time all through the night, as the squalls catch her, the yacht pulls and tugs at her anchor, and then surges forward as she suddenly feels the weight and strain of the tautened cable. Round and round the forestay flies the suspended riding-lamp, and if it luckily escapes going out, or cracking its wirebound globe, is sure to smoke itself black as a sun-glass. Only in the adjacent dimness one little flickering point of light shows where the Dora lies jumping and rolling about in her own uneasy manner; and this is the way in which a rough night is passed on board a small yacht at a quiet anchorage.

Traditionally "gentle" reader, confess that you think this a miserable, wretched, unquiet, unhealthy, laborious way of wasting life, that you are certain you couldn't sleep, sure you would be cold, know you would be uncomfortable and fancy you might be s—— yes, sick! Be it so, and try it all the same.

Steer and sail your own little craft, taking the weather as it comes, never be idle, never heed any qualms, have pleasant companions, a good crew, and comfortable surroundings, get thoroughly tired out and drink a hot nightcap as you go to bed; then if your ground tackle is good, and your boat on deck, free from care you can dream to sleep, and the ripple of water, the pattering of rain, the rattling of ropes and the soughing of the wind, will all fall pleasantly in with the rolling and pitching of the vessel, on your fast forgetting senses, and lull them into a delightful oblivion.

Innumerable are the charms of yachting, which yet interfere not with those of any other sport, and may be pursued even among the toils of a profession. Under his own hand the yachtsman may control the loveliest and most intricate of machines, which nevertheless in the way it is borne upon by accidents of wind and sea, and in its power of rapid locomotion, resembles more the half-sympathetic intelligence of an allied being. His power over it is never complete or assured without the constant exercise of thought and foresight of danger never far away, but which by his unceasing care may ever be successfully averted. He has end-

less occupation and freedom from listlessness. He is
bound to no shore and to no society, but that which
he chooses to carry with him. The purest air, the
clearest skies are his, and from hour to hour, the
forms, the hues which clothe in mysterious com-
binations the elements of air.and sea, are changing
without end before his eyes.

CHAPTER IV.

ST. HELEN'S TO SOUTHAMPTON.

Parting company—A predicament—Southampton High Street—A curious boat's crew—Hamble river.

On Thursday the wind blew harder than ever, and distinctly refused to sanction any attempt on our part to enter the Looe Stream and pass the labyrinth of sunken rocks and shoals off Selsea Bill, which go by the general name of the Owers. Besides, the ship's-company of the Dora were anxious to regain the port of Swanage, and I wanted some stores that could not be conveniently got anywhere nearer than Southampton. So, after breakfast, my passenger deserted me for the schooner, which prudently took a double reef in her sails throughout, while we thought it a fine opportunity to stretch the Widgeon's new three-cornered trysail. Both started at once, but the schooner, with a little more canvas aloft than we, led the way, bruising the seas into scattering spray with her bluff bows, the wind meanwhile bursting down in fitful squalls, with a constant rush of thick rain. Still, everything went

well under the lee of the land, until off Spithead we
met a very nasty sea, and parted company with the
Dora. Circumstances prevented shaking hands, but
they gave us a parting cheer.   Unluckily for us,
we had our topmast aloft, and not expecting any
trouble, had omitted to reef the bowsprit, or even
haul down the bobstay.   Presently, however, the
waves grew so short and high, that we seemed
scarcely off the top of one sea before we were falling
bodily into the next, and frequently had bows and
taffrail under water at the same moment.   Now the
long, pliant bowsprit was reared high into the air,
and now lashing the sea into white water, remaining
buried, until, with a wrench and struggle to get free,
it leapt from under dripping with foam, only to
repeat the performance again with greater vigour
than ever. The topmast would sway forward three
or four feet, and recover itself with a jerk that made
the yacht shiver: the boat which was being towed
astern, would now and again rush at us as though it
would float on deck ; and every instant it seemed as
if something or other must give way. Clinging to
the weather-side of the cockpit, all drenched with
rain and spray, I called to Hescroff, " I don't half-
like this." " No more don't I, Sir!" was the reply; and
not another word was spoken till, after a long and
tedious hour, we were racing down the smooth sur-

face of Southampton Water. Our wetting was mainly our own fault, as the Widgeon would have gone along as dry as a duck with topmast housed, boat on deck, two reefs in the bowsprit, and a trifle more canvas. What amused me in reaching up to Southampton, was to see all the little yachts we met no sooner catch sight of our dripping trysail, than they invariably hove-to, and took in a couple of reefs. About 2 p.m. we anchored off the pier. Rain continued all the afternoon, but did not prevent our going ashore and laying in such stores as we required. The night, which was fairly quiet and fine, passed without incident.

Next morning was characterised by an almost complete absence of wind, and by perpendicular gushes of close rain. It soon became dispiriting to sit in the confined little cabin, with everything around me dripping wet, and nothing on earth to do, since my little world was deprived of the means of loco-motion, and restricted to idle circling round a fixed point—its anchor. Consequently, I told Hescroff to put me ashore, and then made a peregrination under an umbrella which looked like a fountain in full working order, up the High Street, stopping at Wolff's, the flagmakers, to get a burgee, the "Channel Pilot," and a few blue-lights for sudden emergencies in the dark. After a glance at the fine old

D

gate that strides across the street, dividing it into two portions, quaintly styled " Above " and " Below Bar," the weather drove me back in despair, to lunch on board the Widgeon, without paying my customary visits to the yacht-building yards at Northam, and, of course, the moment I set foot on deck, the rain stopped as if by inspiration. Still there was no wind, but, about three o'clock in the afternoon, the very faintest of all possible light airs tempted me into setting a topsail and weighing anchor, in imitation of the numerous craft which were lying still as statues, under clouds of sail, all over Southampton Water. It was a forte of the Widgeon's, however, to sail in a dead calm, and one by one we caught up and passed them. Before we had crept a mile, suddenly a loud hail from a boat, pulling off from the shore, startled me at the helm, and we hove-to and awaited her.

They were a curious crew in that boat. In the stern-sheets crouched a little, slim telegraph-boy: in the bows an old seaman, very broad of beam, was pulling sedately and strongly, but yet, I thought, with a certain quavering unsteadiness. With a lumbering sweep the boat ranged up alongside, and taking a telegram from the boy, I saw a drunken old fellow, who, lifting in his oars with uncertain hands, kept muttering in a low, grumbling key,

"Gimme 'arf-a-crown and 'a done with it, guv'nor. This 'ere's a 'arf-crown job, and a 'ard pull I've 'ad of it, guv'nor. Do now, guv'nor; this 'ere's a 'arf-crown job." Under cover of reading the telegram, which was to the effect that the "Mate" would meet me, if possible, at Shoreham, I had time to examine the old wretch's appearance. His costume was indescribable, although something in the arrangement of its rags and tatters, and in his antique shiny tarpaulin hat, suggested faintly the old man-of-war's-man; but what eclipsed everything was his face. Square in outline, furrowed, wrinkled and dinted with smallpox; toothless, almost noseless, but set with two dark eyes, which would have been bright but for the filminess of age and soddening drink; it was decked all round with scanty, jet-black ringlets of hair curled into little corkscrew spirals with a glittering pomatum. Greedily his cracked and horny fist clutched the bright half-crown which I held out, and glowering on it as it graced one uncleanly palm, he paused a full minute before pushing from alongside, while the other claw gradually overhauled a pocket in his baggy trowsers, extracted a dirty canvas receptacle, and slowly, with shaking fingers, deposited the treasure therein. We turned away, and parting the glassy water with an imperceptible progress, glided past Hythe, past the fine-looking Victoria Hospital on the opposite shore, and finally, after sunset, to the mouth of Hamble river, where we anchored in eight fathoms of water, and spent a quiet night, lulled to sleep by the plashing of rain.

CHAPTER V.

HAMBLE RIVER TO BOGNOR AND SHOREHAM.

Stokes Bay — Portsmouth — Gosport — Spithead — Southsea — Nab
Light-vessel—Dunnose, etc.—Looe Stream—The Brake and the
Pullar—The Owers—The Pilot-book—Anchorage off Bognor—
Owers' Light-vessel—The first watch—Away again !—Little-
hampton Light—Winter Knoll—Worthing—Shoreham—Waiting
for water—Hoisted in the air !

IT was three o'clock on Saturday morning when I
awoke, and looking out of the main hatch in the
dewy dawn, found that the rain had ceased, but there
was not a breath of air stirring. Consequently, although anxious to start as early as possible, in order
to make sure of taking the Looe Stream by daylight,
we were obliged to wait, and had ample time to dress
and breakfast at leisure. A light wind, however,
arose about six o'clock, and in ten minutes we were
under way, with every stitch well set, the anchor un-
stocked and stowed below. The lazy airs in our big
topsail carried us in about three quarters of an hour
to the eastern side of the entrance to Southampton
Water, which was hidden in a thick mist. Then the
tide met us off the uninteresting shore of Stokes Bay,
where the men-of-war test their speed over the mea-

sured mile, and after just fetching the Admiralty Pier about 8 a.m., we were reduced for many hours to short zigzag tacks along shore against a regular Turk of a tide.

One by one, however, Portsmouth and Gosport opened out more and more, every tack by slow degrees brought us nearer and nearer to the frigate anchored off Spithead, the pier and low beach of Southsea came closer and closer, and the sun at last made his exit from behind the ashen-grey clouds, flaming with summer violence down on our dewy decks and sails. Out of Portsmouth Harbour stole a great schooner-yacht, and after a long chase, gradually, very gradually crept past, sailing alongside for half an hour, and giving us a good view of her glistening hull, and the snowy sheets of canvas towering into the blue sky, a hundred feet above our heads. Then, as day drew on, the tide showed symptoms of growing slack, and we edged away for the Isle of Wight shore for a breeze, and to gain the first of the return stream, but near the Nab Light-vessel it fell a dead calm, and all about the Solent were to be seen white shivering sails and upright masts, except far on the westward horizon, where a dark blue line appeared to indicate the presence of a gentle wind. Still the tide was doing us good service, as we perceived by the lengthening out of the high land about Sandown

Bay and Dunnose, from behind Bembridge and Culver Cliff; and when the sun had sunk quite low, and the afternoon atmosphere grew cooler, a light breeze arose, which carried us by five o'clock to the entrance of the Looe Stream. A rapid current seized hold of the Widgeon when she neared this narrow opening between two shoals, the Brake and the Pullar,* which meet here like a pair of callipers, enclosing a space nearly a mile in diameter, with a broad outlet towards the east. We were hurried along like a steamer, between sheets of seething white water, interrupted here and there by the heads of brown jagged rocks, but reduced to mere swirling eddies in our immediate course. The favouring wind and tide in a wonderfully short space of time carried us clear of these and all the other dangers, known under the general name of the Owers, which extend nearly five miles from Selsea Bill seaward.

The Pilot Book says under this heading :— " LOOE STREAM, having in many parts not more

---

* A breakwater might, if necessary, be constructed along the Pullar, for which vessels might run through the openings carrying nearly four fathoms at low water, between it and the middle Owers. The water on the Pullar does not average more than one fathom in depth, so that but little material would be required, and this might be procured not far off, in the Isle of Purbeck, conveyed thence by steam barges, and emptied on the spot. No doubt the suggestion has been often made before.

than sixteen feet at low water, and its west entrance barred by turbulent overfalls, can only be used safely by small vessels, or those locally acquainted. Take care not to attempt it without a fair strong breeze and plenty of time to get through before dark."

Having complied with this wise instruction, and got with safety close to the town of Bognor before sunset, we were looking back on the sharp outline of the low headland with much satisfaction, expecting to make Littlehampton before nightfall, when the wind all at once failed entirely. The tide served us a little further, but its direction taking us out to sea, we brought up in eight fathoms, about three miles off Bognor. The air was perfectly still, and the water smooth as glass. Fishing boats with dark shapeless tanned sails, passed slowly by, and the click of the oars in their rowlocks preceded them by far, and came back with strange clearness from the distance, as they neared the ancient harbour of Pagham, now silted up and rendered useless by reason of shifting sands. At Bognor, where with the naked eye we could count the windows of the tall, bare houses, and with our glasses perceive carriages and people bustling about, there was a brass band playing on the Esplanade, and the notes of its music rolled over the sea to us with a mellowness which they probably owed to the long interval of separation.

Gradually, as dusk drew on, we were left alone on the waters, the band ceased playing, and, although the calm remained still as death, a grim bank of clouds was rising slowly in the southward and eastward. Later still, all the windows of the watering place blazed forth in gaslight, and the flashing lantern of Owers' Lightship was visible astern from time to time, as it threw alternate gleams of white and red.

Notwithstanding the existing quiet, perhaps it was our isolation that made us mistrust the weather, and as matter of precaution, after the evening cigar, take a couple of reefs in the mainsail, house the topmast, reef the bowsprit, and agree to keep watch and watch till morning, so as to be in readiness to weigh anchor and gain an offing on the first symptoms of a change. Mine was the first watch and dull work it was. One by one Bognor lights went out, a little south-easterly breeze began to blow, and the night grew darker and yet more dark, but nothing of consequence happened, and about midnight I called Hescroff and lay down myself.

At a quarter past one, on Sunday morning, the wind had freshened up sufficiently to make Hescroff uneasy about remaining any longer in so exposed a spot, so he roused me and we made sail. The tide against us was now very weak, and although the night was pitch dark, we could get at the bearings of

our course by the flickering gasflare at Bognor and
the regular flashes from the lightship. So long as we
avoided the coast there were no dangers in our path,
and accordingly we resorted to tacks in and off shore,
each of about twenty minutes' duration, steadily but
slowly making way in a fine breeze, which did not at
all increase or vary in strength. A red light, probably that on the pier at Littlehampton, was the first
new object we made out. It appeared on the port
bow and ahead, and we might easily have found the
anchorage, but did not care to do so, as the steadiness
of the wind gave us good hopes of making Shoreham
by daylight. Just as dawn was breaking, we raced by
the buoy on the Winter Knoll, a chalk bank in about
eight feet of water, which we did not perceive until
past it. Wind and tide were now fairly in our favour,
and we were not long in sailing past the low uninteresting shore by Worthing, among the long sea
grass which grows up from the bottom off that town.
Before 7 a.m. we were off the harbour entrance of
Shoreham, conspicuous by its lighthouses and black
timber jetties, and hove-to among three or four
coasters waiting for tide to go in. Not knowing
whether there was water enough on the bar for us to
enter, we seized the opportunity to get a hot breakfast, which the cold air rendered very acceptable, and
after this waited full two hours, in momentary expec-

tation of seeing some one of the signals hoisted, which bristle on the Shoreham page of the Pilot Book. Nothing whatever appeared on the flagstaff, and we were still hesitating, when a paddle tug-steamer, with pilots aboard, came clattering and plashing out of the harbour, and, immediately concluding that where she could go we could, we let go the weather foresheet and steered in. Gathering a fine pace in the freshening wind, with her lee rail flush with the white water, in less than five minutes the Widgeon dashed between the piers, and luffed with a rush into the western arm of the port. Down dropped the foresail, in flew the jib, and the mainsheet was hauled amidships in a trice, when we made fast to a brigantine of some three hundred tons, lying at the Sufferance Wharf.

This was a mistake, since we did not want to go to sea again next tide; for although we had the advantage of lying afloat, instead of aground, we were a mile from the town, and would have done much better to have brought up off Stow's, the yacht builder's yard. However, I did not know this at the time We were soon ashore and exploring the sleepy old village, or town by courtesy, to find its post-office, at which, when discovered, we were unceremoniously refused any letters or telegrams, and obliged to go to the railway station, and seize the opportunity when a train was coming in, to dispatch one or two tele-graphic messages, at about three times the week-day tariff. Then it began to rain hard, and a visit to all the principal inns, or hotels, as they call themselves, failed to disclose any traces of my friend the " Mate," only eliciting the fact that not a single stranger was staying at any one of them. So after lunch I re-turned with Hescroff, who had accompanied me to carry some provisions, to the Widgeon, which to my great annoyance I found partly suspended in the air! The brigantine to which she had been lashed, had grounded with the falling tide, when our little barkie of much lighter draught had still two or three feet of water beneath her. The consequence was that one side was tilted up with the great strain, nearly a foot higher than the other, and part of the rail carried away. Of course we soon released her from that awkward situation, and remained on board. All night rain fell in torrents.

CHAPTER VI.

SHOREHAM TO DOVER.

Stow's Yard—A smash—Brighton—Newhaven—The Seven Cliffs—
Ironclads—Yacht race—The "Cetonia"—Hastings—Dungeness—
Gybing—Folkestone—A wetting—Dover—"What yacht's that?"

THE weather appeared quite fine early on Monday
morning, and I resolved to start as soon as practicable. Stow supplied a carpenter who mended the
broken rail, and also shifted the boom-saddle, to
enable the spar to work clear of the boat's keel, when
it lay bottom upward on deck. While this was being
done, I walked over the little town and bought a
quantity of stores, including some ironwork, which I
got from Stow, whose whole bill came to only five
shillings—an example for Southampton or Cowes.
His yard was full of little craft, amongst which was a
fine twenty-five ton cutter just planked up, and a
number of the Brighton Sailing Club centreboard
boats, built with enormous partly-submerged counters,
to give them greater size for racing purposes than
their measurement would indicate. As the day
wore on, the sky clouded over, and the wind shifted
and freshened, blowing straight down the harbour

entrance, and attended by a little rain. However, as it grew no worse, we ran up the second jib, double-reefed mainsail and foresail, let go the warps, and got some of the brigantine's crew to push us off. They made a mess of the start by giving the Widgeon too much way before we were clear of their vessel's main topsail yard, on which our topmast, although housed, carried away truck and flagstaff about the halliard sheave. This was very irritating, as everything else was in such capital order, for we had just got on board from the railway station the last of our stores, a spare cooking lamp and cans of methylated spirit. Of course the accident did not cause any delay, for we had to tack the next instant to avoid running aground, and then had to go about three times more in the narrow channel between the piers—excessively sharp and anxious work in the jumping sea and shy wind.

There was not much swell outside, and we went along comfortably enough close-hauled, on a course about S. E. half E. for nearly an hour, till at noon we were off the west end of Brighton, which was hardly visible in the mist. Another six miles' sailing along at the foot of the monotonous chalk cliffs, found us off Newhaven, into which harbour we were strongly tempted to run, and I had even put up the helm for that purpose in a thick rain-squall, when the air cleared, and the wind freed us a point or so, enabling us to lay round Beachy Head on the same tack. The tide ran hard against us, and luckily, for the sea was quite as high as we cared about already, and it was a very considerable time before we had left behind the Seven Cliffs, with their curious outlines like consecutive waves, and green blind valleys between. Immediately after opening Eastbourne, which lies on the flat land at the foot of the South Downs terminating at Beachy Head, the wind came on our quarter, and presently nearly dead aft, and the sea increased; but this mattered little, as with her boat on deck (the only time during the whole cruise), and under snug canvas, the Widgeon ran like a witch, never shipping a drop of water. Still our progress through the adverse tide was very slow, and the low coast, only remarkable for a few martello towers, was little worth looking at. In the offing, however, we were accompanied by a whole fleet of merchantmen; I counted forty-seven sail, most of which were full rigged ships, all going eastward like ourselves, with the exception of three immense iron-clads and a despatch boat, which were steaming hurriedly in the opposite direction. Late in the afternoon, we made out far ahead in the mist the tall, gleaming canvas of a large racing yacht, and then three, four, five and more. Soon we passed close under the lee of the first, the splendid schooner "Cetonia," of two hundred tons, taking the head sea dryly as a sea-bird, and leading by a long distance a whole crowd of clippers, the "Gwendolin," "Florinda," "Corisande," "Arrow" and "Lufra." We heard afterwards that she had got the prize, after sailing into a calm, and having to earn all the hard-won lead over again. The match was that of the Royal Cinque Ports' Yacht Club, from Dover to Southsea.

At six o'clock we passed Hastings, and sailed within a few hundred yards of Dungeness Light at dusk, running into smooth water as soon as we had rounded the low headland. Hescroff was for anchoring here, and staying the night out ; but I resolved to hold on, hoping to make Dover Harbour by starlight, as we now at last had the tide in our favour, after sailing ten hours against it. I soon had cause to repent my resolution, for the wind freshened continually, and came so dart aft that we had to gybe no less than six times between Dungeness and Folkestone, to avoid running into stationary fishing boats. The sea grew much heavier, and to add to our difficulties, a dense, thick, rolling mist came down and hid the land, so that I began to fear we might miss the blue light on the end of the Admiralty Pier at Dover, in which case we must either have hove-to all night, or run for the Downs. We made it out however, only just in time, and bowled down towards it at the rate of eight or nine miles an hour. Nearing the head of the pier, which had to be rounded as closely as possible, on account of the strong tide setting across the harbour entrance, I went into the bows to clear away the lashings of the anchor, so as to be able to bring up in a hurry, if required. I had scarcely done so, when there came a cry of "Hold on!" from Hescroff, who was steering. I grasped the shrouds with one hand, the anchor with the other, a great dark mass appeared upheaved ahead, and in the twinkling of an eye all the deck forward was awash with white water, in which I was wetted nearly to the waist. This little surprise was caused by the eddy into which we dashed at full speed when rounding the pier, and which forms a lofty tumbling swell at its point of impact with the true tide. The next moment we were in comparatively smooth water, but so dazzled with the brilliant glare of the gas lamps, with which the pier and town are studded, that we could see nothing whatever ahead, and were sailing blindly on, to the imminent danger of running full tilt into anything that might be in the way. At this juncture a sudden hail came from the pier: "What yacht's that?" "Widgeon!" shouted Hescroff in response. "Where from?" "Shoreham!" "Where for?" "Do—o—o—o—o—ver!" I answered, with

E

an ill-suppressed ejaculation, after which the Customs' officer troubled us no more with his ill-timed questions. A boat with two men rowed up to us, from out of the deep shadow under the town, and helped us to a berth, which we should never have got for ourselves, alongside a little French smack. I looked at my watch, it was past midnight: so after a glass of grog apiece, we turned in, took off our wet clothes, and slept soundly in less than no time.

CHAPTER VII.

DOVER TO OSTEND.

The "Kalafish"—Ostend passengers—The "Ptarmigan"—Towed out of dock—Calm by night—Drifting to Kingsdown—A breeze at last—Cape Griz Nez—Calais—A mirage—Snouw lightvessel—Nieuport—Flight of black ducks—Ostend—"Les Tourments d'Enfer."

IT may be imagined that I did not rise early, after the long tiring run of sixty miles on the previous day, but after a refreshing breakfast of broiled mackerel— a present from the skipper of the French coaster alongside—about noon I went ashore. At the Lord Warden Hotel my friend the "Mate" was discovered at last. He had been waiting there some days, and was very glad to see me, having soon exhausted the sights of Dover. His portmanteau was dispatched at once to the yacht, which Hescroff had in the meanwhile shifted from her night berth into the wet dock. There we found her lying comfortably alongside a little screw steamer, belonging to a gentleman well known in the yachting world, as the inventor and patentee of that nautical curiosity the

E 2

"Kalafish" schooner, which, by the way, came into Dover during our stay. The main peculiarity of this vessel consists in a hollow ram bow protruding many feet under water, the object of which is to alleviate, or even do away with, the motion of pitching. Whether it succeeds in this I cannot say, but speed and beauty are certainly in a great degree sacrificed for the attainment of that end. The steam yacht was fitted with a simple and most ingenious invention by the same gentleman, intended to cast loose a boat lowered from davits, whenever it touched the water.

In the course of the day we were much annoyed, as is often the case near a busy quay, by the dust blowing off the roadway, dirtying sails and decks, and penetrating even into the cabin. This might surely be prevented by watering at this time of year, immediately after the regatta, when the basin is so crowded with yachts.

In the afternoon we walked round by the fleet of elegant hulls, bearing a whole forest of lightsome spars, each tipped with the pretty Cinque Ports burgee. Then came a stroll down the esplanade, followed by a rush to the pier, where a flock of miserable passengers were being shot from one of the Ostend packets. Amongst them I had the pleasure of recognising two or three acquaintances, but very considerately forebore to intrude myself upon them in their too evident distress, and retired to dine quietly at the Lord Warden.

Next morning a new topmast was taken on board, with a stone or two of ship's biscuit, and a gallon of methylated spirit. All was now ready for a start, but having missed the midday tide, we were obliged to wait until night.

As the afternoon drew on, the breeze, which had been blowing for the last week, dropped down to a dead calm, nevertheless we moved the Widgeon alongside a fine schooner yacht, called the " Ptarmigan," close to the dock gates, paid harbour dues, 1s. 11d., (all that was charged us under this head during the whole voyage), and waited in readiness to go out. Evening closed in dark and still, but enlivened by the brilliant lights of the town, which had a pretty effect repeated in the motionless water. On the cliff a military band was playing, at an entertainment of one kind or another, and this was the only sound stirring.

After eleven o'clock, a pilot cutter swept heavily up, and at midnight the harbour tug-steamer took all· three of us in tow, the Ptarmigan ahead, next the cutter, and then the Widgeon hanging on by a rope to her quarter. In this order of procession we glided silently and swiftly through the phosphorescent water between the piers, and cast off on reaching

an offing of a quarter of a mile, the other craft pre-
ferring to give the shore a wider berth.   A hundred
yards more the Widgeon slid ahead, with the
momentum she had gained, and then gradually, im-
perceptibly lost all further motion, except when the
long, low, glassy swell rolled her uneasily from side
to side, swinging the ponderous mainboom forwards
and backwards, until the hull quivered with the con-
cussion.   Her sails held not a breath of air to steady
her, nor was there a noise upon the water, the intense
depths of which glimmered with tiny stars of pale
green light, when I shook the useless rudder.   Away
astern the cliffs of Dover loomed indistinctly in the
moonshine, while from aloft, in the deep dark sky,
like staring eyes of fire, the electric lanterns of the
South Foreland shone down with a steady glare.
Now and again clouds would obscure the moon, and
as one passed, we found ourselves close to a large
brig, with royals and studding sails set, running with
squared yards before a breeze that never blew, up
Channel, towards the Downs.   Then, by a strange
freak, the capricious tide set us quietly and silently
into the neighbourhood of the pilot cutter, with
which we had parted company an hour before.

"Get out your oars!" a pilot shouted, "don't you
see we ain't got no command over our wessel!"

"All right, my sonny!" answered Hescroff, with-

-out complying, but holding himself in readiness, nevertheless, while the two craft, which had approached within twenty yards, drifted slowly just clear of one another, and away.

After a short time the Mate turned in, and soon succeeded in going off to sleep, but I failing utterly, came on deck with the first streak of dawn, and relieved the skipper of his charge. Hour after hour went by and left me idly leaning on the tiller while they slept, my only care being to see that an anchor was dropped, in case we sidled too near the shore; for having no way on, the Widgeon was vaguely heading to every point of the compass in succession, unable to answer the helm. One by one the stars, the moon, and the South Foreland lights disappeared in the dawn, the sun rose, and the land about Kingsdown, a village near Walmer Castle, showed close and distinct, while in the distance the pier at Deal was plainly visible. Beyond it, a fleet of more than seventy merchant-men lay in the Downs, just letting fall the dewy folds of their tall topsails, before weighing anchor. The Ptarmigan, with all her lower canvas aloft, could be descried through the mist, about two miles to the south-east.

At this point the tide turned, beginning, most inconsiderately, to set us back the very same way we came. By seven o'clock we were again, not a mile from Dover, when, as if by magic, a gentle wind came suddenly from S.S.W. I awoke in an instant from a half sleep, and steered for Cape Griz Nez, all weariness vanishing as the delightful breeze bore us quickly over the scarcely rippled green water, sparkling in the morning sun. Before long it freshened sufficiently to awake the sleepers, Hescroff's head appearing suddenly with a most comically puzzled expression out of the forehatch.

Breakfast was next got under way, and by the time it was over, we were near enough to the French coast to be able to distinguish the various crops growing in angular patches on the green downs, the last high land we were to see until we reached the Elbe. The breeze, which had become very strong, was blowing off the land, so that the sea remained quite smooth. We made fine progress, hurrying past Calais Sand buoy at 10.48 a.m., and passing the town itself at 11.18, but not close enough to remark anything but the dark jetties, the tall white lighthouse, crowds of bathing machines on the flat yellow beach, and the masts and yards of ships in the port, appearing over the low sandy dunes.

A more blank and desolate coast it is impossible to conceive, than that of the Pas de Calais and the whole seaboard of Belgium. All that can be seen is a slender line of gleaming sand, here and there tufted with pale green hillocks, and broken, at long intervals, with stacks of tall houses, grouped about a church-tower, or lighthouse. Above, the bright blue sky: below, the bright green sea: only changing in winter to grey and a leaden hue. As for the ocean highway itself, it is dull, and in flat contrast with our busy side of the Channel. Only one old Norwegian barque and a few clumsy fishing luggers met us, throughout the whole day. And little wonder, for a glance at the chart discloses a perfect labyrinth of dangers, in the shape of sunken shoals, with narrow channels between them, hardly practicable for a vessel of burden. Through some of these we now directed our progress, taking a line by compass, from buoy to buoy. To give an idea what speed small yachts, under favourable conditions are capable of accomplishing, I may mention that we sailed the nineteen miles or thereabouts, between Calais and Dunkerque, in two hours and twenty-seven minutes, giving an average of about eight miles an hour. The Widgeon was close-hauled under lower canvas, towing her boat, and the tide was with her.

In spite of the very strong breeze, about noon, the sun had grown intolerably hot; no cloud was above the horizon, and not even the idea of shade suggested by a single tree inland. Our eyes ached with the intense glare on the water, and were played with by a deceptive mirage, so that none of us could sit and steer for more than a few minutes at a time. The beach appeared waving like white breakers in the heated air, and when we passed the Snouw Lightship, within hailing distance, although probably a vessel of two hundred tons, it seemed no bigger than a barrel buoy. Later in the afternoon, as the air grew cooler, the mirage disappeared, and the tide turned when we were off Nieuport, near which we passed a flight of more than a thousand black ducks, which flew unconcernedly quite close to the yacht. Towards five o'clock we sighted Ostend, and arrived there in the midst of a light thunder-shower, accompanied by a blast of wind many degrees warmer than the surrounding atmosphere. The tide had already fallen several feet, and to escape any possibility of running aground, I agreed with two sturdy Flemings, who rowed up to the Widgeon, to give them a few francs for showing us a berth. A strong current set out of the harbour, which gave them a hard pull with us in tow, especially as we nearly ran over them when a fresher puff than ordinary caught hold of our sails. However, they took it all in good part, and well deserved their pay. At 5.20 p.m. we were safely moored alongside the stone quay, just ahead of the Ptarmigan, which had come straight across from Dover some time earlier. Her captain reported that he had the breeze so hard

as to have logged forty-three knots in four hours, and
that they all thought we should have been obliged to
put back.

After dining at the Hotel Royal de Prusse, which,
without a single visitor, seemed a very fair sample of
the whole town, the Mate and I took a walk along
the deserted Digue, (a breakwater of black stone, with
a promenade on the top), and then, after dark, turned
into the marketplace, where a lively fair was in full
swing. Booths of every kind, with fat women, wild
animals, cheap toys, mummies, ginger-bread, and all
sorts of similar delights, completely filled the wide
open space. In a corner, two large merry-go-rounds
were spinning away amid shouts of laughter, to the
sound of fife and drum, not unaccompanied by the
long-drawn sweetness of a barrel-organ. A few glaring
oil lamps cast a dim light on the scene, and enabled
us to descry soldiers of diminutive stature, fisher-
women, servant girls, babies, and boys, mixed up in a
whirl of confusion, as the carved and painted monsters
on which they were seated, came creaking round and
round. Hescroff, who came by at the time, quite
entered into the spirit of the thing, and paid his five
centimes over and over again, like a man, for a series
of revolutions on the back of a wooden rhinoceros,
with a painfully truculent expression of countenance.

As for the Mate, he, too, must have been feeling

a want of excitement, for after a few minutes he suggested going into a booth close by, which attracted our attention by its grotesque adornments of scenes from the nether world, with a flourishing inscription somewhat of this tenour :—" Ici peut on voir les Tourments d'Enfer : premières places, dix centimes ; secondes, cinq centimes."

Could any one resist the temptation of getting beforehand with fate by the payment of twopence ? We, at any rate, succumbed to the eloquence of the lusty charlatan, dressed in a black velvet mantle and skull cap, who strutted about on a raised ptatform at the door, declaiming in the broadest Flemish to a gaping crowd, whose enthusiasm took plenty of rousing. Our entrance was followed by quite a little rush, and when about thirty very respectable-looking people had seated themselves within the tiny canvas erection, the showman came from outside, the green-baize curtain flew up, disclosing a stage about six feet long by four high, and what we saw reminded me strongly of the tragic element in " Punch and Judy."

The audience, unacquainted, as they probably were, with that incomparable drama, took it in quite another light. A hum of sober applause greeted the appearance of at least two dragons and more than four pasteboard monsters and devils comfortably seated amongst flames and rockwork. Suddenly in

hobbled a majestic fiend — horns, pitchfork, tail,
and all ; while to him, at the other extremity
of the stage, entered the King of Terrors himself
— a grizzly being, who towered full eighteen inches
into the air. Here a low murmur went through
the room, and the people's eyes glittered with antici-
pation, when with tottering steps, approached a
wretched mortal, scarcely six inches high. A noisy
harangue from the showman, received with quiet
grins by the undemonstrative audience, and followed
by a wave of Satan's black sceptre, summarily dis-
posed of the poor little gentleman, who disappeared
in the back regions at once, amid a flash of red fire.
After him a clergyman, a market woman, an advocate,
a magistrate, and a fishmonger all went the same way,
till the supply of puppets ran short and the curtain fell.

Returning to the Widgeon, we found her cross-
trees level with the roadway of the quay, and had to
borrow a ladder from the captain of a steamtug, to
reach her decks more than twenty feet below. In
half an hour more the tide left the bed of the harbour
exposed. The moon shining brightly down, lighted
up a wide stretch of unctuous black mud, reeking
with an intolerable stench, which would have prevented sleep, had we not been excessively tired.
Fortunately the sea came in again soon, and covered
up the unsavoury expanse.

CHAPTER VIII.

OSTEND TO BRUSSELS.

En route—Bruges—Ghent—Alost—Place Royale, St. Gudule—Hôtel de Ville—Wiertz Museum—The "Passenger"—Ostend again—A fête—Blessing the sea—History, various—Reminiscences—Story of a commis-voyageur.

FRIDAY morning found us on dry land, bound for Brussels, leaving Hescroff to get the Widgeon's cabin roof painted afresh. Five hours in a slow train gave time enough, and to spare, for passing the country in review, and it was a relief to find it not nearly so tame and uninteresting as it is generally represented. Leaving out of the question the towns of Bruges, Ghent, and Alost, it much resembles any gently undulating, lightly wooded tract in England. What strikes the eye as alone peculiar, is the minute cultivation, which gives a look of gardens to the fields.

We reached Brussels late in the afternoon, and took a fiacre at once to the Hôtel de l'Europe in the Place Royale, where we expected to meet some Cambridge friends, and were not disappointed. The evening, after dinner, was passed in listening to Hungarian music.

Next day we spent in visiting the "lions" of the city. St. Gudule, the magnificent Hôtel de Ville, the Zoological Gardens, and the Musée Wiertz, where an hour was literally wasted among the extraordinary paintings of that eccentric artist. They are all contained in a large room at the rear of an old-fashioned house in the suburbs, quartiér Leopold, not very easy to find. A strange medley of huge wall paintings of Titans devouring men, Gullivers and Brobdingnags, repulsive allegorical horrors, and more literal, more bloody representations of actual war, with here and there a quiet but ineffective portrait. One big picture of the body of Hector dragged opposite ways, in dispute by the Greek and Trojan chiefs, appears ludicrous in the extreme by the disproportion between the heads and bodies. Other more realistic productions are to be viewed only through holes in screens, for the sake of a vivid perspective; but there is only one little picture really worth preserving—a portrait of the artist's mother.

On Sunday our visit came to an end, and the party very unwillingly separated, some leaving for Liège. The Mate, however, myself, and a friend, whom I shall designate in these pages by the name of the "Passenger," who had been invited to accompany us on the cruise, returned to Ostend. Arriving there in the afternoon, we found the whole town keeping a grand ecclesiastical festival. In the morning the ceremony of blessing the sea had taken place, and Hescroff had been much edified by the sight of an immensely long procession, with twelve individuals dressed up in the characters of the Apostles, marching at its head.

I much regretted missing this interesting show, not to be seen oftener than once a year. It is only seldom that the population of such a cosmopolitan watering place as Ostend can be found amusing themselves in their own way. Walk along the Digue or the better streets in August, and in five minutes you will meet as many English, Russians, Germans, French, or other foreigners, as you will native Belgians.

Still, Ostend is not merely a summer resort of strangers, it is also a seaport with a good harbour and fine docks, which would be even more useful than they are, were it not that the entrance is barred with sand. The sea in the offing is also very shallow. This does not, however, interfere with the fishery, in which a great many cutter-rigged vessels of small tonnage are employed.

The town itself does not extend much beyond the fortifications, which are now quite obsolete, but in times gone by have stood a three years' siege, and were only surrendered in 1604 to the Spanish general

Spinola, by express orders of the States-General. Since then the place has undergone many other vicissitudes, as I glean from the ever-ready Bœdeker.

"In the War of the Spanish Succession, after the battle of Hochstädt, Ostend was occupied by the allies under Marlborough. In 1745 Louis XV. took the fortress after a siege of eighteen days, but was compelled to restore it to Austria, by the peace of Aix-la-Chapelle. In 1794 it was again taken by the French, who held it until 1814, after which it belonged to the kingdom of the Netherlands until 1830, when it finally became Belgian in consequence of the revolution."

Strange that all this should pass and leave no sign! but still it is the fact that hardly a remnant of antiquity is to be discovered in the town, most of which is in the condition of being neither quite new nor quite old. Little change has come over it since I spent a summer there twelve years ago. The old King, Leopold the First, then made it his favourite residence; and this, no doubt, attracted prosperity to the place. I used to watch him with childish curiosity in the evenings when he passed up and down the Digue on foot, without show or ceremony, and often unaccompanied. Only by the deference of those who met him and turned out of his path, could it have been surmised that he was a king. Once I saw a tiny little child rush laughing between his legs; he

F

stooped and picked it up in his arms, kissed its frightened face, and set it gently down. This kindliness of manner had much to do with his popularity.

Wherever I walked in Ostend, pleasant reminiscences cropped up, with which I should nevertheless be very sorry to trouble the long-suffering reader. One story, on the other hand, which has no particular foundation in fact, shall be ventured on, with a prefatory apology, because it was told to while away the time one night in harbour at Flushing, to the limited audience of the Widgeon's cabin passengers.

Many years ago, in the early days of railway travelling, a French commercial traveller in the silk trade had occasion to visit Ostend. He put up at an hotel fronting the sea and overlooking the Digue, the name of which, as well as his own, it is immaterial to enquire. His business, for some reason or other, dragged over a period of two or three days, in the course of which events happened that are best described in his own words. He is writing be it remembered, in English, which he but imperfectly understood, to the sister of a lady whom the catastrophe deeply concerned.

"You have demanded of me, Madame, a brief description of the unhappy calamity, of which I have, the week before, been in spite of myself the miserable spectator.

"I am not tardy to fulfil your just demand. There have passed eleven days since that the frightful fate has arrived to me, but nevertheless I remember as if it happened now under these eyes.

"In my capacity of Commis-voyageur, I rendered myself at Ostend with patterns of silk from the part of —— et Cie. of Lyons. In attending that I should have executed my commission, I hired me a bed-room in the hotel ——. To you, Madame, who know Ostend as well as London, it is not necessary to explain the situation of this establishment. This will suffice, that it is not a quarter of a mile from the jetty, which lies along the port, and pushes itself far into the sea. At the table-d'hôte it was, that I first encountered, Madame, both your brother-in-law, and his devoted wife, your sister. We were almost alone at the table, for it was the month of July, when there are few strangers in this town. Your brother-in-law, large, handsome and amiable, addressed me in French; I responded; in a short time we became friends. I did not know then that he was afflicted with a malady of the mind. There was nevertheless a sadness in the sweet blue eyes of your estimable sister, that I did not comprehend. Would that it had never been explained!

"After dinner, the husband and wife retired, but in the evening he invited me to smoke a cigar with him upon the Digue. We went out together. The sun was declining towards the horizon; there had been thunder, but that was all passed; the clouds were disappeared, and nothing was moving upon the sea. The Digue was almost deserted. We promenaded ourselves twice up and down. Then he said, in English, a tongue in the acquisition of which I conceive myself to have made some progress,—'This is dull : suppose I row you in a boat ?'

"I said 'Nothing will make me greater pleasure.' Accordingly we hired us a boat.

"He said 'We will not have a man; I should like to row you about myself.'

"I replied, 'All right!' and because the sun was very hot, I opened my umbrella, and held it above my head. He threw off his coat and hat, and commenced to row vigorously. Excitement seemed to seize him, and he made the drops of water fly from his oars. I said to myself, when I looked at his proportions of Hercules : 'This is a strong man : I should prefer not to fight a duel with him!' Little knew I what should arrive before long!

"In a quarter of an hour he rested, and looked at me, who was smiling underneath my umbrella. Then suddenly he astonished me in saying, with a wild stare, 'Que, diable! What are you grinning at?' The next moment he had recognised his rudeness, and said, 'Pardon me, I was rather excited, and hardly knew what I uttered.'

"He was recommencing to row towards the land, when suddenly a great black 'cochon-de-mer,' what you call porpoise, broke through the still water close to us, with a loud snort.

"The effect was electric! He stopped, looked back after the creature diving away with graceful curves into the distance, and reappearing at regular intervals for breath, and when it could be seen no more, he turned to me.

"'There,' said he, 'There is a happy life! no troubles! no mental or bodily cares! the boundless ocean to live in to all eternity! And yet the sanguinary institutions of man would make it murder to have given to mortal, even though she might be one's own wife, a lot so grandly free! What pity it is, that we must all drown first, and our bodies be desecrated by sharks and crabs!'

"All this he uttered with the most perfect gravity, but bursting into a laugh the next moment, I thought he spoke in jest. Fatal mistake! Even then, had I suspected his madness, I might have prevented the catastrophe of that night.

"Soon the sun disappeared behind the horizon, and

as the moon had not yet risen, it became cold and dark. I closed my umbrella, and begged him to row to land, which he did, conversing quietly all the length of the way, with the cunning of insanity. Arrived on terra firma, he paid the man from whom we had hired the boat double his wage, and then turning to me, proposed that we should smoke still one more cigar upon the jetty. It was fatality! I consented!

"Not a word was spoken between us while we walked along the wooden flooring of the jetty, and seated ourselves at the extreme end. The sky grew darker and darker, and the sea, by consequence, more dim and vague ; only under the town the gas lamps were reflected, in long waving lines of light. A band was playing dance music in front of the Kursaal, the tones of which were wafted over the water to us. Presently that also ceased, and then all was silence. Both of us were smoking like old smokers. How little I thought that the light vapour circling about the end of my companion's cigare, was the last breath of a troubled soul! But it was so.

"The church clock all at once began to strike nine.

"Almost at the same moment, the full moon suddenly appeared, half up the sky, from behind an impenetrable cloud, and to my amazement a fearful change came over your brother-in-law's face. He dropped the last inch of his cigare, threw himself like a savage lion upon me ; and before I was in a state to essay to deliver myself from his grasp, he had bound me hand and foot, with a cord which had been concealed about his person. Never shall I forget the terror of that moment. Fear prevented me from crying out, only my eyes involuntarily fixed themselves upon him, as he stood over me muttering ' The hour is come!'

"Then bending low and hissing into my ear, he whispered, 'Fool! coward! lie grovelling there! Cling to your wretched world! I brought you here to witness how I follow my dear wife in embracing immortality! See!' he cried in a louder tone, dragging me to the brink of the jetty, and pointing to the phosphorescent light that played on the surface of the water; 'See, there lies all of her that was mortal! How the eyes glitter! The crabs have spared them as yet! What was that?'—a distant splash was heard in the water, half a hundred yards away, then all again was quiet,—' I am coming too, Mary!'

"Bon Dieu! how I suffered! Was I then, all helpless, to behold the suicide of a murderer? Thirty seconds passed; how slowly! The madman was listening intently, while I lay motionless and gazing forlornly into the dark abyss.

"Suddenly, but without hurry, from the bottom

arose the body of a giant fish, glistening with spangles of phosphorescent light. Again the splash was heard, as the monster lazily rolled itself half out of the water, and diving in again, betook itself slowly out to sea.

"The madman stood for one moment as if spell-bound; then with a loud cry, 'Mary, I come! I come!' leapt far from off the jetty and fell heavily prone upon the liquid surface. It closed over him with a bubbling commotion, soon swept away by the moon-lit eddies of the falling tide, but I lay helpless to save him.

"Time passed. The church clock struck ten; the cold dew settled upon my body; rats coursed over my motionless limbs; eleven, twelve, one o'clock struck, and then at last came release. I was discovered by the lighthouse-keeper, and taken by him to the hotel, where I have since remained ill and wretched in my bedroom.

"My deposition, Madame, and the full account of all the proceedings at the inquest, you have already had an opportunity to peruse. The only consolation which I can hope you may derive from this miserable recital of the facts, is, that the suicide was manifestly not the act of a sane mind.

"For Madame your sister, it is with unspeakable joy that I have been visited by her angelic presence at my bedside, and that I have thus received ocular demonstration that the madman was but the victim of one more hallucination, in conceiving that he had murdered her who must have been the one light of his fated life."

CHAPTER IX.

OSTEND TO FLUSHING.

Blankenberghe—Heijst—The "Red Sea"—Walcheren—Vlissingen—
Native artists—"Johnny Piloto"—The "Batoo"—"Nae, nae"
—A Dutch yacht—Fishing craft—No dinner!—Bœdeker to the
rescue—"Te row"—Schiedam—Billards à la Hollandaise—Ship
canal—Admiralty charts—"Adam and Eve."

IT was a perfect calm in Ostend harbour, on
Monday morning, when we cast off from the quay,
with every stitch of sail set, but all in vain, for there
was no breath of air to move us. In the end the
Widgeon had to be towed out by two men in a
clumsy flat-bottomed boat. About 9 a.m., when she
got outside, a nice little breeze arose, but dead against
her, and it seemed as if she were sulky and out of
humour with her last port, for she missed stays twice,
probably on account of the mizen being too much
amidships. Unfortunately, too, the tide stood nearly
at high-water, so that little help was to be expected
from that.

Our task soon grew monotonous, the coastline
being even less interesting than that between Ostend
and Calais, not to mention the tediously slow pro-

gress we were making. Presently, however, we were
enlivened by the company of a fine large yacht, bound
the same way with ourselves, the "Seabird," belonging to a French count, but, off Blankenberghe (very
appropriately named, as far as I could judge from the
sea), she had left us far astern, the tide became ebb
and strongly adverse, and the wind softened until it
nearly died away altogether. It is about five miles
from Blankenberghe to Heijst, another little fishing
village and watering place, but six long hours were
spent in accomplishing that short distance. On the
beach at Heijst, throngs of tiny black figures could
be espied in procession, most likely celebrating some
fête, such as that of the previous day at Ostend.

Late in the afternoon, at last, came the welcome
change of tide, and with it a roaring breeze abaft,
which bore us along like a screw propeller. Nevertheless the extreme dulness of the coast scenery,
the cloudy grey sky, and the sea of a sad brick red
hue, for the first time in the cruise made me almost
wish I had not started on it. The suspicious tinge
of the water called forth a hasty cast of the lead,
but that gave the depth as five fathoms. This was
off the Dutch district of Kadsand, in the mouth
of the West Schelde, and the cause of the peculiar
appearance of the sea is, doubtless, earthy matter
held in solution.

Fortunately the depression which had fallen upon us all was not of long duration. Towards half-past five, a smart run of seventeen miles, in two hours, had brought us close under the historic shores of the island of Walcheren. Coasting along at the foot of a green embankment, beyond which nothing of the interior country could be seen, we suddenly shot from behind an obtuse angle into the road of Flushing, or Vlissingen, as the inhabitants call it, amongst anchored ships, fishing craft, and pilot vessels, a boat from one of which immediately rowed up to us.

A pretty sight was the little town, as we hove-to and waited for the boat. The setting sun, just emerging from the lower edge of a dark stationary cloud, lit up, with rays of gold and red, the grim earthworks bombarded by Lord Chatham's fleet nearly seventy years ago. Behind them, large trees partly concealed numbers of quaint picturesque gables, high red roofs, and gaily painted vari-coloured walls; here and there peeping up the bright brown sails of barges lying in the canals, while above all, more than one good old spire rose into the quiet sky. In the foreground, rugged wooden groins of tarry piles intersected the glittering water, against which, nearer still to us, the red caps and russet garments of the pilot crew appeared in pleasant contrast and relief. Over and over again

scenes like this have been fixed on canvas by the old
Dutch painters, Backhuysen, Cuyp, or Van de Velde,
whose pictures by themselves vindicate their perfect
verisimilitude.   However, if it were still needed to
demonstrate how little the artifices of composition
were employed, and how exactly Nature alone was
followed by these native artists, one has only to see,
as we saw it, a town like Vlissingen, literally unaltered
for two hundred years.

The pilot-boat thumping alongside very soon disturbed the general quietude, and then began a lively
conversation in Dutch and English, the only disad-
vantage being, that as all the English was on our
side and all the Dutch on theirs, after several minutes'
talk no one was any the wiser.   At last we gave the
matter up, all but Hescroff, who setting "Johnny
Piloto" at the helm, pointed at the harbour entrance
and requested him to steer the "batoo" in there,
which the man very gravely did, pointing to the sails
every now and then, when something wanted a touch.
Captain Cook must have been quite as intelligible to
the Sandwich islanders, as we were to our guide.   The
only Dutch word in my vocabulary was "guilder,"
but that, with "Nae, nae" (No, no; the spelling, by
the way, is only phonetic), will carry anybody through
Holland.

A few minutes brought us to the narrow passage

between dock gates, which leads into the west harbour, and we were soon securely berthed alongside a
Dutch yacht of about thirty tons, a perfect marvel of
clean varnished wood and polished brass work, but in
almost all other respects like the ordinary schuyt.*
Her bows and stern were to the full as bluff as those of
the old-fashioned Thames barges, and like them she
had leeboards on her sides. Still, notwithstanding these
curious peculiarities, the Dutch craft are by no means
to be despised. After a week spent among their
shallow estuaries, full of rapid currents, quicksands,
mudbanks, and beds of sea-grass, I grew quite convinced that no better type could be invented for
small trading voyages along the coast, varied by
canal work. The largest schuyts draw not more than
about four feet when loaded; if of greater draught
many routes of water carriage throughout the country
would be closed to them. Their rounded bows and
sterns, flat floor and open hold, allow them to carry
the largest possible amount of cargo, even long balks
of timber, on the least displacement, while they are
able to bear a large spread of sail, and are much
faster than their appearance would suggest. Sometimes, it is true, they are liable to upset in squalls ;
but even then, unless the cargo is very heavy, they
will not sink, having no ballast to weigh them down.

* Pronounced " skoot."

Flushing harbour is full of little fishing craft, averaging about eight or ten tons measurement, of build and rig rather difficult to describe, and I am sorry to say I did not bring away a sketch. of one. They are very broad, with low masts and ill-cut square-headed mainsails, fly long coloured pennants, and are often gaily painted, so that a fleet of them presents a very picturesque appearance ; they do not, however, look fit for much real service.

By the time we were dressed in shore "togs," and landed on the quay, the Mate, who strongly objected to lionizing on an empty stomach, having previously consulted Bœdeker on the sly, ostentatiously led the way to the Wellington Hotel, nearly opposite our berth. Unluckily the proprietor was absent, and nothing produced the least impression on the servant in charge. First of all I tried the simple word "dinner," in four or five languages, with variations in pronouncing, cunningly devised to hit the Dutch appetite, but it was of no use ; she simply stared and said, " Nae, nae." At last we grew desperate, especially the Passenger, who gesticulated with a faculty of invention for which no one had given him credit, in the vain hope of expressing the idea of hunger to that unflinching woman's brain. The Mate said nothing, he only pointed to his mouth. What was to be done ? Just as we were thinking of carrying the larder by storm, Bœdeker came to the rescue, mildly suggesting in half a line of small print, "Hotel du Commerce."

We took the hint and went there. The proprietor understood French, and in a quarter of an hour a maid set before us a dish of the most underdone beef-steaks it has ever been my fortune to behold. Of course it had to go back to the fire, but how to convey that notion to the girl was again a problem.

"Es ist zu roh!" I said; she stared, and gradually broke into a smile, but I persevered ringing all possible changes on monosyllables beginning with R, till a glimmer of comprehension lighted up her face, and with a surprised mutter, sounding like "te row!" she snatched up the dish and departed. In ten minutes it came back beautifully done. Bewilderment gave way to hunger now; but when a bottle of hock was brought in, and our glasses filled with a mysterious observation every time, the Passenger grew much affected. He conceived that the simple maid, following some mediæval custom, was invoking a saint's blessing on our wine. I thought so too, but had not clearly caught the name of the saint. However, the Mate, who after the first surprise had been listening quietly, said it was no such thing; the words were "As you please," or something like it; and so it afterwards turned out.

When dinner was over, we tasted Schiedam, in wine-glasses, with bitters. The impression it created was not a very pleasant one ; and we certainly did not expect to get accustomed to it in less than a week, when first we sipped it in the intervals of " Billard à la Hollandaise." Leaving the Mate and the Passenger immersed in a game, with three-inch balls, and untipped cues as massive as crowbars, I took a walk and communed with a cigar on the ramparts. Under the statue of Admiral de Ruyter, who was born here, I met Hescroff, who with the unfailing instinct of seamen, had already discovered a compatriot. This was a Mr. Simmons, a ship and boat-builder, the son of a former Mayor of Poole. Though born and bred in Flushing, and speaking Dutch like a native, one could still discern in his clear but slightly hesitating use of English, a tinge of the Dorsetshire dialect. He was a most obliging man, and offered to show me over the town, an opportunity which I was glad to embrace.

Whilst walking round to the East Haven, he informed me that he and about thirty others were now the last remnant of an English colony, once nearly 1500 strong, who with the help of a few German Lutherans, still support a Presbyterian church. Amongst themselves they seldom use the language of their adopted country, although many

of the children at least must have lived all their lives
in Holland.

Passing some large empty ship-building sheds,
deserted warehouses, and a tiny war vessel, nothing
more than a sloop-rigged coaster, mounted with two
six-pounder guns, the only representative of Dutch
naval power, we reached the new docks. What a
contrast they presented to the picturesque antiquity of the other parts of the town!

It is a really great work to have dug such a harbour
for ships, out of the solid plain, to a depth of twenty
feet and more, and to have fenced it round with deeply
and thickly driven piles, on which courses of the
smoothest and most accurate looking masonry are
laid, every stone fetched from distant foreign lands.
But this is not all, a broad ship canal of equal
depth traverses the whole island, uniting the waters
of the Ooster and Wester Schelde, and supplanting
the natural channel between Walcheren and South
Beveland, which is now bridged by the railway* from
Bergen-op-Zoom.

---

* Is it too much to expect that the Admiralty charts will from year to
year recognize alterations of this character, which are matters of common
repute, and scarcely need ocular verification? The chart of the river
Schelde, bearing date May, 1872, only indicates the railway by a faint
dotted line, with the words, "Projected, 1867." The consequence was
that had we not visited Flushing, we should have gone miles out of
our way, only to be stopped by the bridge, and having to come back

Great efforts have been evidently made by the Government to develop the port ; but the commercial activity which the inhabitants were expecting, at the time of our visit appeared a thing of the future. Some weeks before, we were told, one large vessel had passed through, and there certainly was a little Dutch yacht lying in the dock, and a turret ironclad in the canal ; but with these exceptions, when the Widgeon entered it next day, hers was the only flag that broke the monotony of the scene.

The solidity of their construction is the most striking quality of all Dutch works. This was well exemplified in everything we saw around us, but more especially in a small trading sloop Mr. Simmons pointed out to me in the West Haven. It bore the name of "Eve," and the respectable antiquity of a hundred and fifty years. Originally, two were built, "Eve" and "Adam," but after thirty winters "Adam" came to grief, leaving his widow behind, a silent standing rebuke to modern "coffin" ship builders.

Arriving at the Widgeon, I found her sitting upright in the bed of soft mud at the bottom of the harbour, which is very shallow, and only to be entered by vessels of five feet draught, about an hour before

again. It is impossible to keep pace with the changes of quicksands and shifting banks in the Dutch rivers, but such things as an important railway ought to be noticed.

and after high water. When the last few inches of the ebb had drained away, the smell became very overpowering, but our experience of Ostend, which is much worse, carried us through the night without a murmur.

CHAPTER X.

FLUSHING TO MIDDLEBURG, TREVEEREN, AND OVERFLAKKEE.

Peter van Petegem — Middleburg — Stadhuis — A turret-ship — Treveeren — A sketch — The Schelde — Duiveland — Tholen — "Polders" — Zijpe—St. Philipsland — Dutch country-house— Bruinisse—Krammersche Slikken—Overflakkee.

THE early tide was lost in getting provisions on board and hiring the pilot, Peter van Petegem, who had been recommended to me by Mr.Simmons. It was agreed to pay him thirty shillings for a week, or any less number of days, within which he might bring us to Amsterdam. The old fellow came on board with a heap of testimonials from English yachtsmen who had appreciated his services, and he quite deserved the one I gave him when he left us. He could speak broken English, and stood very good-humouredly much chaff about his pipe—the German china bowl of which was nearly big enough to hold his kit. About four ounces of tobacco replenished it in the morning, and it was lighted, smoked, and extinguished several times in the course of the day. Luckily tobacco, such as it is, can be purchased in Holland for about a shilling a pound. The face of the bowl was adorned in gilt letters, with "Peter van Petegem, geboren 1811." I asked him if he was born with it in his mouth? His little grey eyes twinkled as he answered, "Nae; I die wis."

We could not sail out of the harbour until nearly five o'clock, though a shallow centre-board yacht, called the "Eugenie," of nine or ten tons, belonging to a Belgian gentleman, left an hour earlier, for Ostend. Once outside, however, a fine light breeze took us quickly into the East haven, and after a delay of a few minutes at the lock gates, occasioned by our having absolutely no papers on board to prove the Widgeon to be a yacht, we were admitted into the dock. A sail of half a mile brought us to the canal entrance, and there we were taken in tow by a great rawboned horse, the wind being adverse, otherwise we might have sailed.

On either side of the canal high banks conceal the country, and as it is of modern date, no houses are built upon them, so that the whole length is rather devoid of interest. The only amusement was to watch the quadruped in charge of us. If he had not been broken-winded, broken-kneed, and afflicted with string halt, people might have been found to say, that although not what is called beautiful, he was a useful animal, with plenty of bone (he certainly had that)

and good muscle. N'importe ; he served his purpose; taking us over the four miles to Middleburg
before dusk ; for which the driver received three gulden, about five shillings, and rode away against the
sun, like a rustic Death, on his charnel steed.

Petegem, the Passenger, and I rowed up to the
town in the Waterbaby, racing on the way some fair-
haired little urchins in a clumsy boat, who called after
us " Goodnight," as we left them astern. With only
an hour to spare, not much could be seen, but, sending
the pilot off to engage a second horse for the last five
miles of canal, we made the most of our time, and
passing down three or four gloomy red-brick streets,
found ourselves on a sudden face to face with a
splendid building, the " Stadhuis," or town hall,
built by Duke Charles the Bold of Burgundy, in
1468, in Late Gothic architecture, of light-coloured
stone. The lower story, full of tall mullioned windows with pointed arches, appears only simple and
grandiose ; but the story next above is elaborately
beautiful, with its row of similar windows intermixed
with salient niches, containing fine carved figures of
the Counts and Countesses of Zeeland. Between
them and the eaves, delicate Gothic tracery springs
from the wall in strong relief, and, higher still, rises a
massive roof, pierced with innumerable dormer lights.
This roof is relieved at either end by turreted gables,

and, at one corner, by an octagonal tourelle, with a richly-ornamented balcony, rising in several stages from the ground. Dominating the whole composition stands a square tower of great size and majesty, dividing at the angles into four pinnacled turrets, which are reunited by flying buttresses to an eight-sided erection in the centre, surmounted by a dome and weathercock. Nothing in greater contrast with the substantial, low, burgher-like dwellings which surround it, than this tall and graceful fabric, can be conceived. I had just time to buy a photograph and make some necessary purchases, including a pound of tobacco for Peter, before returning to the yacht.

On our way back we passed the huge grey-painted ironclad turret-ship, which I have alluded to some pages back, lying in the canal close under the windows of the town. Thus the fifteenth, seventeenth, and nineteenth centuries all had their true representatives here, in the Stadhuis, the houses of Middleburg, and the modern vessel of war.

By the time we were fairly under way, in tow of a sturdy horse, it was getting quite dark, but we pushed on, as there was nothing to meet in the watery road lying straight as an arrow's flight before us. At half-past nine the final halt was made, the horse-conductor paid off, and he soon clattered away out of the feeble circle of illumination thrown by our anchor lamp

TREVEEREN, ISLAND OF WALCHEREN.

[To face p. 80.

from the forestay. Groping about in the dark, we came upon the sea gates of the lock, and there met its keeper, a retired master mariner, who talked English with us for a few minutes, and kindly promised that his subordinate should let us out as early as possible next morning. One or two seamen belonging to some barges alongside, came down and admiringly fingered our delicate blocks and ropes, and after a vain attempt to open a conversation with us, retired. Then all was quiet.

It was about four o'clock A.M. when I awoke, and with the aid of Hescroff and Peter, hauled the yacht through the lock and set sail, drifting clear of the canal mouth in a light northerly air. Outside the groin, the boom was allowed to swing over on the starboard side, and we ran away very slowly before the wind. Veere, Treveeren, or Kampveer, as I have heard it differently called, lay right astern, and seemed a large place in the cool, grey, morning mist, lightly touched by the pale rays of the rising sun. Our advance was so slow, that I was able to make a sketch of the scene, to which a capital foreground was afforded by two schuyts with tall sails running in our wake. It must be taken *cum grano.*

Just as I finished my drawing, something or other awoke the Passenger, who jumped up on deck in a very confused state of mind, and wanted to know where he was. It was no sooner explained to him than the Mate also caught the restless contagion, and had to be quieted in his turn; after which came breakfast.

The arm of the sea in which we now found ourselves is called the Veer Gat, and has a general southeast direction for about a mile, up to the entrance of the Zuid Vliet, which trends easterly, between the islands of North and South Beveland, passing eventually into the Engelsche Vaarwater of the Ooster Schelde. This is rather a monotonous bit, as but little more of the island scenery can be discerned than here and there a red roof among the tops of trees appearing over the green embankments. Nothing living bore us company, for the schuyts were bound another way, only here and there a silent solitary stork was to be seen probing the mud shallows, in quest of fish. The channel is rather narrow and tortuous, though well buoyed, and as the wind shifted, we had once or twice to tack. Peter Van Petegem soon showed that he thoroughly well understood the set of the currents, as well as the dangers in our course, and without him we could not have got over the distance between Flushing and Amsterdam, nearly so quickly as we did. Only a light topsail breeze was blowing, which failed us entirely in Zand Kreek, where we were forced to anchor for two hours, waiting for the change of tide.

Towards ten o'clock a nice little breeze arose, and, with everything set, we soon beat up the Engelsche Vaarwater, rounded the buoy off the northern end of the Galgen Plaat, and, slacking sheets, ran slowly up the Keeten Mast Gat, between Duiveland and Tholen. Here, again, little of the country was visible. It lies extremely low, large portions of it having been from time to time submerged by the sea, while others, like Anna Jacoba land, for example, are reclamations of no ancient date. These "Polders," as they are called, lie often many feet below the surface of the water, and have to be jealously defended by strong dykes. Internal drainage, after these embankments have been constructed, is effected by a series of waterwheels.

A month or so might very pleasantly be spent among the islands of the Maas and Schelde, whose quaint old towns would, I am sure, well repay exploration. As it was, we had no opportunity of landing to examine the curious drainage works, canals, and dykes; fortunately at Brunsbüttel similar work was going on, which we were enabled thoroughly to inspect. Towards noon the sun became very hot, and killed the wind, as the sailors say, till there was not sufficient for us to stem the tide. Consequently we had to anchor again, between Duiveland and the little isle of St. Philip, off a steamboat pier at a small town

called Zijpe, a word which our pilot wrote and pronounced "Seip." Close by the shore at St. Philipsland stood a large country house, looking for all the
world as if it had come straight out of a Vander
Heyden picture. The chart alludes to it as the
Witte Huis (White House), but probably it has some
other name. Presently, from a distant harbour, presumably Oude Tonge, in the island of Overflakkee,
three or four miles ahead, came a clean, white-sailed,
centre-board boat amid a fleet of schuyts, and dis-
tancing them all, soon passed by us on the strong
favouring current. About six o'clock a light breeze
tempted us to trip the anchor, and make the most of
the tide, which divides off Zijpe two hours after low
water. Leaving under our lee the little fishing town
of Bruinisse, with its crowded harbour and forest of
low masts, we tacked, and soon weathered the dangerous quicksands of the Noord Plaat, where large vessels
have before now been completely engulphed in one
tide. From this point the wind was fair, and carried
us quickly on to an anchorage, off a shoal called the
Krammersche Slikken,* on the south shore of Overflakkee. No human habitation was visible anywhere
near, so we supped, smoked, and retired to sleep
early, without attempting to land on the uninviting

---

* "Slik" is Platt Deutsch for "mud."

mud. The wind blew hard all night, but off the land, so that there was no sea.

The Widgeon had brought up with a tremendous jerk on the anchor; the tide racing past at the rate of at least five miles an hour.

It is, of course, this force of currents, and the number of shallows, narrow channels, and quicksands, which render the navigation of the Schelde and Maas dangerous to those not locally acquainted.

CHAPTER XI.

WILLEMSTAD TO DORDRECHT AND ROTTERDAM.

Hollandsch Diep—Inundation of 1421—Moerdijk railway viaduct—
Rembrandt's Mill—A Glimpse of Dort—Fellow-countrymen—
Watering—Rotterdam—" Boompjes "—Bric-à-brac."

AT eight o'clock on a beautiful bright morning, we
set all sail close-hauled to a very soft wind, and passing the fortified city of Willemstad, the ramparts
of which date from 1583, turned into the broad
Hollandsch Diep, an estuary of the Maas, robbed from
dry land by a fearful inundation in 1421. Beneath
its waters are said to lie sanded up the ruins of
seventy populous villages, and the skeletons of a
hundred thousand human victims, but nothing in its
present aspect recalls that harrowing memory. On
either side lie the inevitable flat green shores, but they
appeared more dotted with signs of life than any
we had seen hitherto. Many miles in the distance
ahead, loomed up the huge railway viaduct* across
the Diep from Willemsdorp to Moerdijk, with its

* Although this bridge was finished in 1871, my Admiralty chart,
published in 1872, gave no indication whatever of its existence, yet it
purported to contain *corrections* up to the latter date.

fourteen iron arches of great spans; and about
eleven o'clock, we sailed into the narrow Dordsche
Kil, close to that splendid piece of engineering
work.

The Kil, though salt, is little more than a canal,
and its low banks are covered with verdure, trees,
and houses. Towards the northern end, a number of
large and very picturesque wind saw-mills mark the
vicinity of Dordrecht. Despite their antique appearance, the dates borne by most of them are within
the present century, yet in external aspect they
exactly resemble that in Rembrandt's lovely etching,
—his father's mill on the Rhine. Each has a name
of its own, boldly set forth in large characters and
often brilliant colouring; "Fortuna," "de Twee
Gebroeders," "de Drie Kronen," "de Vrouw Helena,"
and the like. Schuyts and barges also, which we
now began to overtake literally by scores and
hundreds, for we could outsail them all, bore similar
curious appellations carved in gilt letters on their
sterns, above the little square cabin-windows decked
with pots of flowers.

Quite pleasant company are these quaint craft
with their family crews, who keep them with incessant
scrubbing, bright and clean as yachts, and look upon
them as their only homes. Occasionally we passed
a schuyt with as many as four generations dwelling

on board; the old great-grandmother shrivelled as Lachesis, her daughter, the fat vrouw of fifty, the rugged owner of the craft, her husband, his married eldest son, wife and tiny child. More often only one young couple, with a host of chubby urchins, find room in the confined low cabin, where it is wonderful that they can stow themselves at all.

Among a crowd of these companions, the Widgeon reached the railway viaduct near Dordrecht, about the middle of the day. There she had to wait until a train had passed, before the custodians of the swinging-bridge would let her through. My chart, as usual, quietly ignored the presence of any such obstruction. Soon the Mate and the Passenger grew tired of the delay, and pulled off to the town in the Waterbaby. Almost directly they were gone, the bridge opened, and sailing through, we stood off and on among a tangle of shipping, which gave us much trouble sometimes to avoid a collision. The waters of the Oude Maas appeared quite alive with the little steamers from Rotterdam and the country round, hurrying about with scant regard for anything in their way.

Just as I was admiring the line of grim tottering red-brick houses domineered over by the hoary Cathedral tower, in deep contrast with the river's modern animation, Van Petegem suddenly became

restless and uneasy, delivering himself of some inscrut-
able utterances in broken English. Hescroff at last
interpreted them to mean that if we delayed even a
few minutes, the tide, which we were already scarcely
able to stem, would prevent our reaching a point
half a mile ahead, whence it would be fair to Rotterdam. Consequently, as there was no time to
spare, I was reluctantly compelled to leave behind,
without a visit, the old historical city and its unper-
pendicular tower, so often painted by Cuyp in the
backgrounds of his sunny cattle pictures.

The tide was all but master of the situation and
the issue of the struggle hung for many minutes in
doubt ; but at last, reaching our goal, we hove-to in a
narrow green-bordered channel which communicates
with the Nieuwe Maas. In a short time the Waterbaby joined us, her crew thoroughly exhausted with
the hard pull against the stream, under a broiling sun ;
and then we proceeded. The breeze would not allow
of our sailing through, except by holding on close-
hauled until we fell too near the leeward bank, and
then shooting up in the wind's eye, to fill off again for
a long reach until the manœuvre was again required.
There was no room to tack, but the tide standing our
friend, we made good way in the manner just described. A fine schuyt with a large and well-cut new
mainsail, luffing as close to the wind as we could, gave

us much trouble to overtake, but before two miles was gradually passed.

At a village called, I believe, Oostendam, an English brigantine was unloading. This vessel had cleared from Poole some time since, and on being hailed by Hescroff, her skipper and crew gave us good luck, evidently rather astonished at meeting so small a craft so far from home.

Sailing out of the canal into the Nieuwe Maas, the river banks appeared thickly covered with villages, fine trees interspersed with gaudy pleasure houses, picturesque shipyards, and all the paraphernalia of commerce. Steamers of all sorts and sizes crowded the way, and the country barges were almost innumerable, dotting the winding reaches like flights of ducks. The water on the ebb was fresh enough to drink, and we laid in a store for both tanks, Peter averring, " Dat de best vatter in Holland."

Just after this we glided past a pretty summerhouse, open towards the river, in which a Dutch gentleman, his wife, and several children sat playing with dogs, books, and musical instruments, exactly (costumes excepted) as they are represented in countless old stiff and formal family portraits of the seventeenth century. Our trim little yacht, of strange build, with the British red ensign flying at her mizen, attracted their attention at once, and they all ran forth with exclamations to watch her out of sight. It was about five o'clock when we anchored off the dark red brick houses and clustered yellow masts of Rotterdam, the second city of Holland, and a most important commercial port. Far as the eye could reach, large barques and full-rigged sailing ships lay busily loading or unloading at the long-stretching quays, and scattered in among them huge American liners, London, Hull, Grimsby, Leith, Newcastle, and Antwerp packets, in their respective berths, jostled with little tug-boats and screw launches which ply daily to Gouda, Dordrecht, Hertogenbosch, Middelburg, Arnheim, Nymegen, and Brielle. Blocks of warehouses, towering story upon story high, front the Maas, leaving broad gaps here and there, where the canals run backwards into the town. Chief among these are the Leuve-haven, the Oude-, Nieuwe-, Scheepmakker's-, and Wijn-havens, and the Haring-vliet, nearly all crammed full of brightly-varnished hulls, with tall pennon-flaunting masts. Every few hundred yards, where the carriage roads intersect and cross the canals, rise drawbridges, with vast horizontal beams poised in the air among serried rows of bushy green trees, which mask unpleasing features and add colour and variety to the scene. Towards the west, a grand viaduct carries across the Maas the same railway with which we had previously come into contact at Wal-

cheren, Moerdijk, and Dordrecht.   Beyond this lie
the quays called "Boompjes" (from the trees planted
along them), and Willemskade.

The general form of the town is that of an equi-
-lateral triangle, having its base towards the river, and
nearly bisected by the Hoog Straat (*High*, not *Hog*,
Street), built along an embankment about a mile and
a half in length.   Thither, on landing in the boat,
we threaded our way through narrow streets, by no
means as clean as usual in the Netherlands.   A few
minutes were spent, en route, at the shop of a gold-
smith, whose window was full of old silver trinkets,
and the Passenger, somewhat of an amateur in bric-
à-brac, bought for a few shillings the quaintest of
little antique teapots, daintily wrought in miniature,
and standing about two inches high.   The vendor,
who spoke a little English, directed us to the Victoria
Hotel, in the Willemsplein, whither we repaired after
visiting the Groote Markt, which is built on vaults
over a canal.   Dinner followed as a matter of course,
and afterwards the novelty of Rotterdam soon exhausted itself, and we were glad to find ourselves on
board the Widgeon, once more, ready for a start
the next morning.

CHAPTER XII.

ROTTERDAM TO GOUDA AND TOLLHUIS.

Early morning on the Maas—Life on the Canals—Gouda—" Brigga-houaloo ! "—Fall of the Meerschaum—Mosquitos.

BY five a.m. interrupted work was already recommencing on the busy river ; little steamers began puffing about, and the occupants of schuyts came tumbling out of bed, shockheaded and sleepy-eyed, to their matutinal ablutions. Presently three or four very large barges caused us no little uneasiness, by weighing their anchors and helplessly drifting with the stream in our direction. When at last their dwarfish guardian, in the shape of a tiny screw tug-boat, had fairly got its flock together and begun to move away, snap went the tautened rope, and off sidled the barges—at us again ! Keeping a hard hand on the tiller, we just sheered clear of them ; the steamer came to the charge like a sheepdog, and finding her bound our way, we hailed her for a tow : that is to say, Van Petegem settled the matter for us, in screaming guttural Dutch. The little insignificant screw, hardly as large as the Widgeon, trailed two enormous cables, one on each quarter, to each of which eight clumsy schuyts attached themselves one after another, and we brought up the rear of all.

It was nearly nine o'clock when we bade farewell to Rotterdam, and slowly wended our way at the tail of this procession, among the larger shipping. Big drops of rain plashed on the decks, and for a while the sky wore a grey, forbidding aspect. However, an hour or two later, after passing Kralingen, its guard-ship and salmon-fishing apparatus, all on a sudden the sun shone out in splendour, chasing away every cloud and adding glorious light to an already warm, quiet day. It was delightful to lie on deck, just lazily touching the tiller, smoothly, without exertion, borne along the glassy surface of the stream, between fair winding banks, here bordered by beds of green rushes, there topped with umbrageous trees clustering about some fine old mansion, whose flower-garden extended even down to the water's edge. Slow as our progress was, one after another we passed all the schuyts sailing in the same direction, their bright tan-coloured or white sails picturesquely breaking the view.

It grows so hot that we are driven to dress in white flannel clothes, and rig up an awning over the cockpit. Van Petegem produces the china pipe, and the Mate smokes, in tacit rivalry, a splendid meerschaum,

which came back with him from Brussels. Feeding
time begins and appears likely to last long, for on
these lazy river craft there is little else to do. We
pass a schuyt with four rosy, chubby children, the
oldest not yet six, all seated round an earthen pan full
of potatoes fried in fat, sticking them on sparsely
pronged steel forks, and eating away with the zest of
out-door life, while papa and mamma look on amused.
Our especial cynosure is a large, clean, handsome
schuyt, immediately astern of which we are being
towed along. On board of it the old father takes
turns at steering with his lanky yellow-haired son of
nineteen, while the mother and young sisters are
busily occupied in shelling enormous beans. The
girl, who is really quite pretty, keeps looking up to
stare at the strangers in the yacht, but the old vrouw
soon gives her an angry box on the ears, and makes
her turn her back to us and shell beans without any
intermission, for a long half-hour. Whereupon the
Passenger lights a good cigar, and says "It's a horrid shame;" and I think so too, but begin to get
jealous and look askance at the Passenger, who
doesn't notice it a bit. So I also stifle my feelings in
the fragrant weed, and we broach a cask of Rotterdam
beer.

Next we are hailed by a sunburnt peasant, who is
anxious to be allowed to tow us with his horse to

Amsterdam, since the steamer does not ply beyond
Gouda. Fourteen gulden, he asks, but Peter beats
him down, after ten minutes' of nasal wrangling,
to a dozen only (about £1), and he leaves us to cut
across the country to his idle steed. We meet him
again, mounted on a sorry beast, at a sharp bend of
the river, when another unintelligible parley ensues ;
then he mysteriously disappears, and we see him no
more until Gouda displays itself, already well on in
the afternoon.

This town has a population of 16,000 souls, a
manufacture of bricks and clay pipes, and several
interesting antiquities, of which the most renowned
are the forty-four stained glass windows in the Groote
Kerk, executed about the close of the sixteenth
century, many of them by the brothers Dirk and
Wouter Krabeth. However, we did not land, only
stopping a few moments at the drawbridge to pay off
the steamer* and attach a tow-rope to the quadruped
we had engaged instead. So it happens that my
memory of this town is quite as fugitive as the
Claimant's could be on occasion. All I recollect is,
that the Yssel is there thickly overhung with trees ;
and that, having pitched a stray copper coin or two
among children to be scrambled for, some of the
little vagabonds ran by the river side for a mile or

* The charge was 8s. 4d.

two after us, and were only stopped at last by a deep
ditch, bridgeless and full of water.

Indeed the sweltering heat, the constantly changing
scenery, and the novelty of being towed through a
strange country without any exertion of our own, were
so delicious that we felt for a season quite overcome,
and could scarcely summon energy to ask the pilot
so much as the names of places. Even when we did,
his extremely broken English would not decide any
difficult point either one way or another, and spelling
was not an art in which he had attained proficiency.
Consequently, to this hour, I remain in blissful igno-
rance, and cannot tell precisely by what canals we
journeyed, and what villages we passed through, during
those two delightful days between Rotterdam and the
capital. Villages there were by tens and twenties,
each with its drawbridge for communication between
opposite banks, on approaching which, our driver
would utter a loud yell, sounding like "Briggahoualoo!"*
prolonging the antepenultimate with a most unearthly
shriek. This always brought a tollman out of his
little house in a hurry, to stare at us first, and then
vigorously set to work at the machinery for raising
the beams and roadway. While this was going on,
a little crowd would collect, of market carts and foot-
passengers of all kinds, just as one may see at a rail-

* Quære? " Bridge ahoy ! "

way-crossing in the country at home, when the gates are shut for a passing train. Then for a few minutes we were under the curious inspection of the crowd of idlers, till we slowly shot through the narrow passage with the momentum we had preserved, and regained the unfastened tow-rope on the further side. In passing through, the tollman or his wife would always extend to me a tiny bag at the end of a long pole, into which the customary fee of twopence had to be smartly placed. After sunset this payment increases to a penny a head, and at one place Peter was actually asked in Dutch whether we had any one stowed below !

For a considerable distance beyond Gouda the canal, or canalised river, winds incessantly and often almost back upon itself, so that the direct progress made is not more than half the number of miles traversed. The country is pretty and well wooded.

My notes mention that we passed a place when the twilight was already falling, which must, I think, have been Zuid Waddinxveen. There the horse took a little rest, and a mile or two farther on, we entered a long straight reach of still water, full of floating weeds. On either side the banks were darkly overhung for a long distance, with bushy overgrown trees, the sun had gone down, and our anchor light was glimmering on the forestay. A singular quiet pervaded the air, and except ourselves, no traveller was disturbing the still deep water, only here and there a solitary fish, large and heavy, would leap with a sounding splash at some ill-fated fly.

Suddenly there came a cry from the Mate, who had carelessly let fall his meerschaum of great price into the canal. Fortunately it floated, and a hasty pull of a hundred yards in the Waterbaby, restored it to the anxious owner.

Another mile of towing brought us to a little place called Tollhuis, where is a wretched country inn. The Widgeon was made fast to the bank, the horse led away to feed, and then Petegem followed the Mate in a search for beer. They came back with a jarfull of a sour thin beverage, flat and bodiless as ditch-water,* which only Mr. Peter delighted to honour; and it was relinquished entirely to his use. But the worst was to come. Scarcely had we composed ourselves to sleep, when there was a great commotion in the water, fearful earsplitting shrieks from a steam whistle, and then a long screw steamer, carrying a flaring red light on her bows, passed us after the double warning, at arms' length distance. Air and water were scarcely still, when the cabin began to resound with humm, m . . . . . m . . . . .

* Amstel beer is a fair native brew; Beijrsch (Bavarian) beer i also to be had in most places, and good.

m . . . . . humm, mm . . . . . m . . . . . m . . . . .
in a tremulous minor key, like the long drawn murmur of a tuning fork.   Never had I heard that note
before ; but in a moment it flashed upon me that we
had fallen a prey to the fell mosquito !   A severe bite
at the back of the neck in a moment confirmed the
idea, and then we all began to realize what is misery !
I wrapped myself entirely up in a woollen railway
rug, leaving no aperture even for breathing, and so,
by good fortune, succeeded in deadening the still
small voice, and staving off any further attacks.   But
the discomfort of the remedy almost equalled that of
the disease.   As for the Mate and the Passenger,
they slew right and left—the cabin panelling was
plastered with victims in the morning—but what
were these among so many ?   Sleep, the daughter of
the gods, at last made our troubles light, but I shall
remember Tollhuis as long as ever I live.

CHAPTER XIII.

TOLLHUIS BY THE RHINE, THE AAR, AND THE AMSTEL TO AMSTERDAM.

Fruit for Covent Garden—Post at Waalsdijk—Bædeker—Paleis van Volksvlijt—Petegem and the "Musketeers"—A Cambridge "Grind"—Table d'hôte—Mixture of nationalities—Dutch customs—Jewesses—An old Dutch lady—the Damrak.

RISING with the sun, we started in the cool fresh air of the dawn, and crossed "de Oude Rijn" at about six o'clock. If I remember rightly, the river is not more than about a hundred yards wide at this point, and there are four locks, one at each cardinal point of the compass. The landscape scenery is pretty and picturesque, clumps of rich dark green trees alternating with villages of gaily painted houses. Was it here or further south, on the previous day, I forget, that we met whole crowds of schuyts, laden high and heavily with round baskets, open at the top, and filled to overflowing with the most luscious of cherries, transparent ruby currants, early gooseberries, and the latest strawberries of the year. All this luxuriance of fruit was trending in one direction, that of Rotterdam, and in all probability some would be shipped thence for England, to reappear at old familiar Covent Garden.

Leaving the Aar, and entering the Upper Amstel, a considerable increase was noticeable in the breadth and depth of the channel ; indeed Van Petegem assured me that only in long droughts was it impracticable for a vessel drawing eight feet to follow our route. The course of the river is, however, very winding, and sharp corners are frequent. Round each, of these are stationed curious posts, fitted with rollers and guards at their tops to prevent the tow-ropes from flying over them inland. One of these erections, near a place called Waals-dyk, I sketched as we hastily passed it. The guard, which prevents the rope from leaping over when the horse jerks it by breaking from a slow pace into a trot, was in this case made of iron. From its upper extremity projected a rude representation of a skeleton hand, roughly welded out of iron rod.

It was not often that we could see far inland, but now and then the banks lay sufficiently low to enable us to perceive long stretches of meadow pasture, dotted with trees and innumerable black and white cattle, and every mile or so intersected by a deep ditch or a low rampart of earth, besides innumerable drains. Again I found it almost impossible to write down the names of the hamlets by which we were journeying, although we must have paid a few minutes'

visit (among many others) to Oudshoorn, Vrouwen-
akker (of which I have a faint remembrance), Uithoorn,
and some places unmentioned in any of the maps I
have seen, which in general are very faulty with regard to the courses of rivers and canals. Bædeker's
are nevertheless good and sufficiently trustworthy,
considering their small scale, and his whole book of
Belgium and Holland a most useful work, of conveniently moderate dimensions and price.

At nine o'clock we reached Ouderkerke, which Peter
called and spelt " Oulkerig," and waited there a quarter of an hour, while the horse had a feed. Beyond
this the river widened more and more, and the country
for many miles around opened out under our eyes,
until between ten and eleven, after passing a quaint
old house called Ooster Meer, we caught a first
glimpse of Amsterdam.

That famous old city appeared in the distance one
mass of red roofs, intermixed with spires and windmills, and lightly veiled by a thin translucent canopy
of smoke. The elegant glass dome of the Teutoon-
stelling, (Exhibition building) however, dwarfed all the
rest, and glittering in the sunlight, appeared like a
kingly palace, which we at first understood Van
Petegem to mean, when he called it " Palais van
Volksvlijt.* An hour later, after twice running

* Palais d'Industrie.

aground, and being forced to set sail, since the shallows near the banks prevented any more towing, we anchored off the great Amstel hotel, but on the opposite side of the river.

Whilst dressing to go ashore I had a short conversation with Hescroff.

"How did you get on last night?"

"Well, sir, I got famously bitten by them there musketeers; but it was nothing to what Peter got!"

"How do you mean?"

"Why they bit him so he couldn't stay down in the fok'stle; up he jumps on deck, and when I put my head through the forehatch there, I could see hundreds of them creatures flittering about the anchorlight; so I just pulled down the hatch and fastened it inside—and Peter, he staid out all night!"

"Well, and what happened then?"

"Oh, I got off pretty well scot-free after that, but they insects got under Peter's clothes and stung him till he could hardly sleep a wink."

This accounted for his taciturnity all the morning. Before noon we were all ashore, except Hescroff, who was left in charge of the Widgeon, and the unhappy pilot pursued his vocation on dry land, where he was, metaphorically speaking, at sea. By dint of incessant questioning, however, and engaging a fly, we made pretty rapidly for the Bijbel Hotel in the Warmoes

Straat, the back windows of which look directly down upon a canal called the Damrak. There the simple-minded old Peter van Petegem was paid off, with a small present in addition to his wages, which evidently made him happy as a king. I regretted having to part with him, as he never grumbled, and always went honestly to work according to his light. Further, however, he could not guide us, and so departed, in the joy of his heart, to spend the afternoon with Hes-croff, before availing himself of his railway ticket back to Flushing.

After lunch, we all came to a tacit agreement not to attack the curiosities of Amsterdam, at least that afternoon ; but, fatigued as we were by the early rising and scanty sleep of the four previous days, only to drive leisurely down to the yacht, pack up a few clothes for immediate use, and return to the table d'hôte at half-past four. Before reaching the Widgeon, to save a long drive round, it became necessary to get out of the carriage and cross a canal upon a floating pontoon working backwards and forwards with a winch and cogwheels, on a chain lying down at the bottom. The whole machine was nothing more nor less than what is called at Cambridge a "Grind." I had thought "Grinds" were indigenous to our own soil, but now the surmise grows upon me that some son of Holland may claim the invention.

I

Talking of nationalities, the people who sat down to dinner with us at the table d'hôte, were certainly as heterogeneous a collection as could well be imagined. Close to me were sitting a party of three or four Dutch gentlemen, apparently habitués of the place, who confined their conversation to remarks upon the dishes, and confidential orders to the waiters. On the opposite side was placed an English commercial man, and his young wife, who said hardly a word the whole of dinner time. Then there were a couple of seedy-looking Frenchmen, who fully made up for the general silence by their volubility and gesticulation; a little shrivelled old German, and lastly, a grey-haired yellow-faced Creole, evidently rich and still more clearly ill at ease, who never opened his mouth, except to eat. One tie only seemed to unite them all—business. Besides the Mate and the Passenger, I think I did not come across a single individual travelling in Holland for pleasure alone.

The dinner, which consisted of several courses, was fairly good and not expensive. At dessert we were rather surprised to see the men all take out cigars and cigarettes, and begin to smoke, without even asking the lady's permission, but afterwards found it to be the custom all over the country.

In the evening, accompanied by a commissionaire who understood English, we went to a concert at the

Paleis van Volksvlijt, or rather in the garden attached.
A lively crowd of people, in every class of life except
the highest and lowest, were seated there round little
tables, drinking Beijrsch beer or lemonade, smoking,
and listening to a capital brass band, which was playing military music in a covered orchestra. The
generality of the audience were common ordinary
people, whose fresh and somewhat countrified looks
might easily pass muster in any small English pro-
vincial town. Here and there, however, among the
fair-complexioned Hollanders, were sprinkled black-
eyed, black-haired Jewesses of a strange cast of
beauty, playing with children, miniature images of
themselves. This being attended so late at a public
entertainment by their young sons and daughters,
was itself a clue to their race; for the Dutch, *pur
sang*, dispatch their babies early to bed, as we English
do. In one corner of the garden sat a handsome
old lady, conspicuous, although she seemed neither
to challenge nor desire it, far beyond the rest. Her
fine, firm face, clear and bright although wrinkled
with age, her well-arranged dazzling white hair, and
general distinction of manner, made a *tout-ensemble*
which breathed the spirit of another century, and
declared a higher rank. It was not until a second
look, that the quaint and rich peculiarities of her
costume claimed attention. She was plainly dressed.

in deep black silk, disclosing only here and there the little appurtenances of snow-white linen, which incomprehensibly complete the feminine toilette. Instead of gems, she wore a heavy chain and bracelets of smooth, solid gold; but what lent the distinctest character to her appearance were two thick, round, convex plates of the same precious metal, one on either side of her forehead, partly concealing it, and themselves overlapped in part by the folds of a white headgear, the exact form of which I totally forget, nevertheless, at the time, it pleased me. Whispering a question to the guide, he answered, *sotto voce*, " She is a Friesland lady of old family, but you must not think that all Dutch ladies dress like that ; it is a country custom, and quite out of fashion in Amsterdam." "The more's the pity," I thought, and said so, but he only smiled incredulously, and then began to descant on the decadence of Holland, evidently a pet theme with him.

"Ah ! the country was in a bad way ; there was no life, no spirit. Foreigners stepped in and took trade out of the very hands of old Dutch merchants. Why, only the other day, an Englishman came over, when they wanted waterworks at Amsterdam, and offered the leading commercial men to supply part of the capital, and let them have it all their own way with the direction of the enterprise. That was a safe affair! But they half-promised and hesitated, and half-promised again, till he drew back in disgust, and allotted all the shares abroad, and now there were those waterworks making ever-so-much per cent., and they might have all realised fortunes, instead of losing them in South American securities. He had just seen an old family, one of the oldest and once one of the richest in Holland, off by ship to their East Indian estate, ruined, positively ruined by speculation in rotten foreign funds, when they might have got safe interest out of much-needed home investments. If capital was wanted for any native enterprise, it was impossible to get it, while millions were at once subscribed and lost upon any glittering ephemeral project from abroad. It was enough to make a man despair!"

He ran on like this until it was time to go. The same story is heard everywhere among the lower classes in the towns; but I am very far from believing that, even if it has some real foundation with regard to the losses of leading commercial families, it is true respecting the general wealth of Holland. It does not take at all into consideration the increasing wealth of the middle classes—the agriculturists for instance—who, for many years past, have found a ready market in England, at high prices, for all they could possibly produce. This very circumstance, indeed, has raised the price of meat, butter and cheese in Holland nearly to an equality with what it is among us, and consequently the pockets of all the classes, of which our commissionaire and his family were a fair example, are seriously affected, and their minds drawn towards despondency.

Doubtless people of all ranks live more luxuriously now than ever before in Holland, as elsewhere, except perhaps the leaders of society, whose magnificence is not so overt as it was in the old times, when the few who were rich were very rich indeed, and recorded the fact in lasting monuments, which, still existing by the side of modern makeshifts, tell to imaginative minds a tale which is not borne out by other testimony. In spite of all possible eulogy of the old magnificence and wealth of Holland, I believe the country never, during its whole existence, was so well off in every way as it is now. It has declined, not positively, but only relatively to other countries, which have passed it in the race of civilisation.

With these thoughts I entered my bedroom at the Bijbel, opened the window slightly, as it was a hot night, and retired to bed. In a short time the horrid stench of Ostend and Flushing filled the room; the Damrak, on which my room looked out, was a perfect sink of filth, and the water in it very low. Yet Amsterdam is considered a healthy place!

CHAPTER XIV.

AMSTERDAM.

Dutch Sundays—Israelites—Diamond cutting—Rijks Museum—Rembrandt's "Night Watch"—Van der Helst's "Arquebusier's Banquet"—Museum Van der Hoop.

THE Dutch, as a general rule, fall short of us in the strictness of their observance of Sunday. As for the Jewish portion of the population, Saturday is, of course, their day of rest. They generally work a few hours on Sunday morning, and then take another half-holiday on the afternoon of the Gentile Sabbath.

A careful study of Bœdeker, and a conversation with our commissionaire, determined us to pay a visit this day to the Jews' quarter, the Rijks Museum, and at least one of the famous diamond-cutting factories ; the latter first, for reasons which I have just mentioned, the workmen being nearly all Israelites.

We were taken to a large dingy house in, I think, Zwanenburger Straat, and entering by a narrow side-door, walked up a gloomy winding staircase into a large room, from whence the hum of voices and the buzz of machinery was heard as we approached.

Nearly three hundred rather ill-favoured and dirty-looking individuals were sitting around, before each of whom lay a rapidly revolving metal disk, covered with oil and particles of diamond dust. These disks are worked by leather endless bands from two metal shafts running from wall to wall, just below the ceiling, and set in motion by a steam-engine on the ground-floor. Each workman had also by him five or six curious-looking objects, more like life preservers than anything else, little sticks with large knobs of lead at one end. In each of these knobs a diamond is embedded, leaving only the side exposed requiring to be polished: the sticks are then fixed lightly by their plain ends, and the weights of lead are allowed to press the diamonds gently against the revolving disks, which gradually wear them down. In another room are a number of models of celebrated diamonds. In going out I asked how the workmen, if inclined to be dishonest, were prevented from stealing and making off with the precious gems entrusted to their care. The answer was that if any stone disappeared unaccounted for, the whole body together would be obliged to pay the full value; so that they would all have a strong interest in discovering the thief. Collusion to defraud is thus rendered next to impossible.

From the diamond-polishers we bent our steps to

the Rijks Museum,* and found there much more of
interest. In a few badly-lighted rooms are displayed
more than five hundred pictures, amongst which are
the very finest examples of native art.

I suppose no one ever visited this collection for the
first time without walking straight up to Rembrandt's
" Night Watch," and stopping in front of it to work
up the requisite admiration for a picture so world
renowned. It stands conspicuously in the middle of
the first room, on a level with the eye of the spectator, challenging the criticism of close inspection,
brazening out a claim to be valued above everything,
defying cavils—almost entreating them. Of this I
felt all the effect, and yet a sense of disappointment
crept over me. Can a painter's work be good and
true when it portrays a scene of broad sunlight, as
colourless and black in shadow as it might appear
under the faint glare of a solitary tallow candle ? Is
not there an obvious disproportion in the central
figures, and a want of dignity that is ill compounded
for by liveliness of incident and bold contrast of light
and shade ? So much, I fear, has to be admitted ;
nevertheless, the famous canvas must not be denied
all credit for wonderful artistic vigour and power,
though many a smaller picture by the same great
hand, to me has appeared in its characteristic merits

* State Museum.

equally, if not much more beautiful, with defects either actually fewer, or else, by sinning on a smaller scale, less patent and obvious.

That very title, the "Night Watch," which has clung to the composition for more than half a century, is a misnomer, although an excusable one. The whole area, fourteen feet by eleven, is alive with a mass of figures representing a company of civic arquebusiers coming forward into the light of day, from their lofty dark Guildhall. Attired in deepest black, their captain, Frans Banning Cock, marches first, and beside him Willem Van Ruitenberg, the lieutenant, who in his yellow tunic bears a little more life-like, martial air. More in the background, steeped in gloom, stand the drummer and flagbearer, with a straggling crowd of rank and file.

Such is the celebrated "Night Watch." Now let us turn to its noble rival, the "Arquebusiers' Banquet," by Bartholomew Van der Helst. If the name of that great painter has not yet commanded its due meed of praise, this picture, nevertheless, by its own inherent beauty, inspires the acutest feelings of delight. Of its kind, I imagine, the world cannot show its equal ; it is the triumph of portrait art. Better-handled pens than mine have before now striven in vain to do it justice. Perfection will not be described.

Painted, they say, to commemorate the celebration

by the Arquebusiers of Amsterdam of the Peace of
Westphalia, at a banquet held in the summer of 1648,
the huge canvas places before the eye a crowd of
richly dressed martial figures, beaming with jollity
and good-humour. On the right hand, before a long
table groaning with good cheer, Captain Wits, distinguished by his rich black velvet attire, clasps by the
hand Lieutenant Van Waveren, while the other lifts a
silver cup of wine. In the middle, the stout old
ensign, Jacob Banning, sits encircled in the flowing
folds of his cherished flag ; and even the maid-servant,
who is entering with another dish for the banquet,
shares the universal look of gay contentment. Won-
drously true to nature, and yet never vulgarised, is
every detail. The hands, if possible, are more life-like
than the heads, and the inanimate objects appear as
if they might be stolen away and put to use. The
colouring is quiet and rich, but not heavy. As for the
scattered light, which has been complained of as a
defect, why it is the pride of the composition : it is
the soul of that animation, that apparent carelessness
under which lies concealed the truest, noblest, most
laborious art !

All pleasures have an end. After these two the
other pictures in the gallery appear commonplace by
comparison, although many are gems in themselves.
We spent a considerable time in going conscientiously

through the rooms ; but that day I could admire nothing more.   Leaving the Rijks ·Museum, a few
minutes' walk took us to the Van der Hoop collection, where there are some fine pictures by Jan Steen.
The other galleries we had no time to visit.   In the
evening, after the table-d'hôte, I went with our commissionaire into the Jews' quarter, and reconnoitred
the canals through which the Widgeon would have
to pass the next morning, before reaching the Zuyder
Zee.

CHAPTER XV.

AMSTERDAM TO THE PAMPUS.

The Ij—Mud navigation—An accident—English schooner yacht—
Aground—Off again !—A Netherlands man-of-war—Overhauling
charts—Hints for cruisers in Dutch waters.

IT is not nearly so easy to get a yacht out of, as
into, Amsterdam. No fewer than seven bridges inter-
vene betwixt the Widgeon's anchorage in the Amstel
and the Oostelijk Dok, which communicates with a
large expanse of water called the Ij,* through a lock
traversed by a swinging railway-bridge. The Ij,
again, by another magnificent lock, affords access to
the Zuyder Zee.

A stevedore was engaged to pilot Hescroff through
the intricacies of this inland navigation, and to assist
him in poling the yacht along the town canals, which
are so shallow that I really believe her keel was often
trailing through the soft liquid mud at the bottom.
All the morning was occupied at this kind of work,
while the Mate, the Passenger, and I were driving

* Pronounced like "eye."

about and purchasing comestibles for the voyage. It was half-past two in the afternoon when we at last met the yacht emerging from the canal, her iron cross-trees bearing the traces of an encounter with a very narrow bridge, where they caught on both sides, and were symmetrically bent several inches backwards. This I was rather vexed at, but made no attempt to remedy until we reached the Elbe, and could have recourse to a blacksmith. Dutch craft having no topmasts, altogether dispense with crosstrees, and so I recommend any one to do, in traversing the canals. All topmast gear is much in the way when a draw-bridge does not rise quite fast enough, or where trees thickly overhang.

With much difficulty, in hardly any wind, we beat under sail against a slight current, up the Oostelijk Dok, and shaving by a few feet only the jibboom end of the corvette guardship, soon found ourselves in the vicinity of the lock gates. There it was necessary to wait another couple of hours, while train after train rumbled over the swinging bridge ; but at last that ponderous machine moved slowly aside, and we hauled into the Ij.

The pilot steered our little vessel with evident satisfaction at her speed and handiness, down the narrow ship channel which leads out of this wide shallow lake. He was anxious to be allotted the same office on board of her in a regatta which was to take place about a fortnight later, but had to be told, much to his disappointment, that we could neither wait until then, nor come back in time. However, even if we had been able to do so, it is not likely that we should have greatly distinguished ourselves, for I noticed lying in the Amstel one or two very smart-looking American centreboard craft, much better fitted than the Widgeon for racing in water so smooth and confined. A small schooner yacht, belonging to an English engineer, was at anchor in the Ij, and we were told that she often sailed in the matches, but was not successful.

Just as we were scanning her with critical eyes, the Widgeon, without any shock, slid gradually to a standstill in a bank of soft mud, and there stuck for at least half an hour. When we got the anchor out astern, and hauled on the cable to get her off, our biggest "mudhook" divided the half-liquid slime like a ploughshare, and suddenly re-appeared under the counter. With much trouble, owing to the difficulty of reaching any bottom to push against, we extricated our distressed beauty from her toils, by means of a long pole, and set sail again just in time to reach the lock before sunset.

Close in our wake the guardship, a large old wooden corvette, was parting the glassy waters in tow

of a fussy little steam-tug, and we sheered on one
side to let the monster pass. Her bulwarks were
crowded with naval cadets, and their officers, in the
background, appeared almost as much interested in
us as the boys. But the greatest excitement came
when we were safely lodged in the dock, alongside
the huge vessel, that might have carried the Widgeon
slung in davits, without feeling her weight more than
a feather. The fair-haired, rosy-featured sailors were
in ecstasies with the Waterbaby, handling her tender,
smoothly-varnished planks and lifting her half out of
water, surprised to find how stiff, and yet how light
she was.

Of course the Netherlands man-of-war was not kept
long in waiting, and we reaped the benefit of her company, by being let out within a few minutes, just as
the sun was dipping below the red horizon. The
stevedore was paid off, in spite of his repeated entrea-
ties to be hired as pilot for the Zuyder Zee; and we
hurriedly made sail, with the intention of making the
corvette our guide into open water. However, she
anchored after proceeding two or three miles, and we
followed her example at dusk, getting a fright by
nearly running over a boom, that stood up from the
bottom like a warning skeleton finger. A hasty cast
of the lead reassured us, the depth being nearly two
fathoms, but we did not care to go any further, as the

night was cloudy and there were signs of wind. Our anchorage rejoices in the odd name of " Pampus."

After dark, Hescroff and I spread the chart of the Zuyder Zee on the cabin-table, and with rule and compass laid down courses for the morrow, by the light of the flickering candle-lamp. All appeared plain sailing on an E.N.E. line, as far as the tiny little island of Urk, which occupies a very central and isolated position ; but beyond that the inland sea is one mass of intricate shoals, with hardly any depth of water over many of them. In fact the prospect could not be considered reassuring, and we retired to rest with very lively wishes for a fine morning and a fair breeze. In this I am glad to say we were not to be disappointed. Ever since leaving England, the weather had been only too calm and hot. From the night we were towed out of Dover harbour to our first arrival in Hamburg, a period of nearly four weeks, only two or three passing showers of rain molested us, and there was hardly a day during the greater part of which a large topsail could not be carried. Later on, upon one occasion only, we were to experience a little wind and sea in the Elbe, but that was when our cruise had virtually terminated.

The calmness of the weather was the more acceptable, because we had started almost without any definite plan, and in many parts of our route, any un-

K

expected and strong adverse wind would have caused
great inconvenience. As it happened, however, although we rarely had any idea where the Widgeon
would be the next week, or even the next night,
favouring breezes generally brought us to some quiet
port at the close of day, and the slight uncertainty
was pleasant enough, so long as all turned out well in
the end.

Our voyage, as a whole, was probably never made
before by any English yacht, or other craft. Vessels
of such low tonnage as the Widgeon seldom or never
go so far afield, and on the other hand it is safe to say
that many of the canals and shoal passages which we
traversed, would be inaccessible to yachts of larger
dimensions.

One of the few drawbacks to our enjoyment, was
insufficient cabin accommodation, and this difficulty is
not easily to be got over, without materially increasing the size and water draught of the vessel. In fact,
there is only one way to obtain a comfortable cabin,
and still keep the power of navigating safely the intricate shallows of the Dutch coasts, and that is, by the
use of a centreboard keel.

It would not be difficult to design a cutter yacht
fitted with this contrivance, which, with a draught of
only three feet, would measure less than twenty tons,
and contain a cabin with six feet head room or more.

Such a craft, about thirty-six feet long, by twelve feet beam, would possess a very high degree of stability, and by placing her lead ballast very low and making the centreboard of galvanised iron, might be rendered uncapsizeable. She should have a slight rise in the floor, a full round easy bilge, and not too heavy bows or run. She would be capable of beating to windward well, without the use of her sliding keel, and could cross nearly all the shoals of the Zuyder Zee. As for her speed, it would be very fair, and she would be an excellent sea boat. Four roomy berths might be obtained in the cabin, and there would be a great deal of room in her forecastle for the crew, as well as plenty of space for a cockpit and sail-room aft. Lastly, in bad weather there would be few harbours for which she could not run at any state of the tide. I commend these hints to the attention of any one who may undertake to repeat the " Cruise of the Widgeon."

CHAPTER XVI.

THE PAMPUS TO ENKHUISEN BY THE ZUYDER ZEE.
Islands of Marken and Urk—Enkhuisen—Medemblik—Stavoren—
Legend of the Vrouwen-sand—Fishermen—Enkhuisen Harbour—
The Westerkerk—Architectural curiosity—" Mulluk."

THERE were not many evidences of waking life on
board the man-of-war, as we passed her in the grey
of the morning, afrer weighing anchor at half-past
seven. All sail was hoisted, but the light wind
hardly moved us at the rate of more than three miles
an hour. As the day drew on, it brightened, and the
breeze displayed a little more strength, but it was
past nine o'clock before we brought the lighthouse at
Marken to bear a little west of north, and left our
anchorage of the previous night five or six miles
astern. Marken has for its capital a small fishing
village, of quaint wooden houses, inhabited by a
people who dress in a costume of their own. The
history of the place has been full of vicissitudes, and
the neighbourhood is worth a short visit, but as we
were in such a hurry to get on, it had to be left for a
more favourable opportunity. So we steadily pursued our lonely way, over the smooth sea unbroken

by a single sail, except where our sleepy companion,
the corvette, was lingering still at anchor. In a few
hours more, the coast line became scarcely visible on
the horizon, we sighted the island of Urk, a mere
speck on the water, in the distance ahead, and the
sun became quite oppressively hot, so that the awning
had to be put into requisition. Urk, as we neared
it within half-a-mile, about noon, looked exactly like
a town built in the sea. The land is so low as to be
hardly visible, and the picturesque red houses and
little church tower seem to huddle together on the
highest spot, like people caught by the tide and afraid
of wetting their feet.

Mr. MacGregor, who visited this diminutive country
in his canoe, " Rob Roy," a few years ago, writing a
letter to the *Times*, with an account of his cruise,
gave some interesting details concerning the population, who do not, in all, number two thousand souls.
Yet, as it appears, they are self-supporting, and the
administration, almost purely local, might be a model
to that of many more important places. In the
winter it is often impossible for the country-craft to
reach the island, on account of the roughness of the
sea, and then, if not always, Urk is a little world in
itself contained.

At 2.45 p.m. we had sailed considerably to the
northward of this odd little Utopia; the tide had

turned against us, and on hauling up the patent log, which had been put overboard at 9.26 a.m., it was found to mark a progress of twenty-six miles. We now tacked and stood to the westward, in the direction of Enkhuisen, off which town the increasing wind compelled us to take in the topsail; and then, opening Medemblik late in the afternoon, by six o'clock the Widgeon had worked as far north as Stavoren, on the eastern shore.

All these three places in early mediæval times, and even later, were commercial cities of wealth and importance, but have now lapsed into poverty and decay. Sundry evidences of ancient riches, however, despite their present squalor, hang about them still, and the interest which they excite is augmented by uncertainty as to the causes of decline. These were probably many and continuous, but not startling in their operation; the popular impression seems to be that the cities fell through arrogance and extravagance, insensibly working internal ruin. However this may have been, Enkhuisen, which once contained forty thousand inhabitants, who owned four hundred fishing vessels, and from among whom sprang Paul Potter, the celebrated painter, now lodges but five thousand in its grass-grown streets of tenantless houses, and frowns upon an empty harbour. Medemblik is a poor fishing village, but Stavoren,—the tale of Stavoren is the most romantic of all. It has been told so often, that I shall simply quote Bædeker :—

"The ancient Stavoren, the city of the heathen god *Stavo*, the Thor of the Frisians, is now an insignificant place with only five hundred and seventy inhabitants. It was once the residence of the Frisian monarchs, and at a subsequent period a wealthy and populous commercial free city, the third in the celebrated Hanseatic League. Its vessels are said to have been the first which passed through the Sound, and its naval enterprises prospered as early as the twelfth century. Old chroniclers relate that the citizens of this favoured spot were in the habit of employing pure gold for many purposes to which the baser metals are usually applied. Thus the bolts on the doors of their houses, the rivets and fastenings of their yachts and pleasure-boats, and the weathercocks on their churches, are said frequently to have been made of that precious metal. The town is now a very poor place, not even possessing the means of rescuing its handsome church-tower from the ruin that threatens it. The decay of the place is chiefly attributed to the fact that the harbour is gradually becoming filled with sand and thus rendered useless. The Vrouwen-sand,* a broad grass-grown sandbank in front of the harbour, derives its name from the

* Lady-sand.

tradition that the wife of a wealthy merchant once desired one of her husband's captains to bring her from abroad 'the most precious thing in the world.' The worthy Dutch mariner, in conscientious fulfilment of the request, accordingly brought back a cargo of wheat from Dantzic ! The lady, indignant at his stupidity, ordered the valuable freight to be thrown overboard at the mouth of the harbour. This act of wanton waste ultimately caused the ruin of the proud and luxurious city. The grain is said to have taken root, and to have formed the foundation of the sand-bank, which is daily increasing in extent, and constitutes an insuperable barrier to the entrance of the once excellent haven."

Nothing, I believe, except the grass bank, remains to corroborate this touching story, and perhaps that will not be accepted as evidence sufficient.

We were all somewhat anxious to go ashore at Stavoren, but as the wind blew quite fresh from the N.W., with a nasty short sea, and there appeared no quiet anchorage, we were reluctantly obliged to seek shelter for the night under the lee of the other shore. In less than sixty minutes our little barkie was quietly anchored in smooth water, a few hundred yards from Enkhuisen, just as the sun went down.

This antique city presented a very striking appearance of a semi-oriental character, full of quiet repose.

There lay a deep shadow under its high sea wall, green with luxuriant grass, and topped with a dense grove of shady trees, above which peered housetops and lofty gable ends reddening in the dying light, while over all towered a strangely beautiful church spire.

. Before our sails were all stowed, two fishermen in a rough awkward flat-bottomed boat, pulled off and boarded us. They had a pail with about thirty little flounders in it, which I bought by signs, for tenpence in Dutch money, after the usual vain attempt at conversation. Then it occurred to me that fresh milk, eggs, bread, and beer, were luxuries not to be despised by the adventurous mariner of seas unknown: so I jumped into the Waterbaby, and Hescroff pulled her after the retreating Hollanders. They very considerately waited for us, and showed the way into the harbour, nearly a mile from our anchorage. The inner basin, which was unoccupied, except by one or two smacks, is entered by a narrow channel between piles, which appear to have been lately renewed. Leaving our boat under the care of our guides, who were charmed with its delicate fittings and light build, we passed through the fishing quarter, into the better part of the town. Several fine old red brick mansions of the seventeenth century met our eyes, but the streets were half empty and over-grown with grass. Many houses were decaying for want of repair, and more were tenantless, or inhabited by people of a lower class than those for whom they evidently had been built. No good shops exist, but I succeeded in discovering a small photographer, whose pretty daughter sold me a view of the fine old Westerkerk, although we had no two words in common to bargain with. In the course of our after-peregrinations, Hescroff and I were much amused at a curious relief in plaster, fixed on the quaint gable of a schoolhouse. It represents a furred and bearded pedagogue, in the act of birching a refractory pupil, and is vividly painted to the life.

Soon twilight began to grow apace, and hurrying back towards the harbour, we had the good luck to pick up a young fellow, who without knowing a word of English, was wonderfully quick at understanding signs, and attached himself to us uninvited, in the capacity of guide. The news of our arrival had spread like wildfire through the town, and we were followed from shop to shop by an enthusiastic crowd of admirers, consisting chiefly of small boys. In marketing, our quasi interpreter was very useful, and without him, we should have been hours getting over difficulties of the most ludicrous kind. One old woman offered us clothespins for matches, and salad-oil for milk. In fact it seemed as if we should have to go away without the last mentioned article. " Milk," " milch," " melk," " malk," " mulch " were all tried in vain, till a

THE WESTERKERK, AT ENKHUISEN, ON THE ZUYDER ZEE.

[To face p. 138.

saturnine bystander suggested, in a tone of half apology, something like "mulluk," whereupon they looked at one another and fetched a panful, thickly covered with delicious cream. At last everything was collected, and we headed a noisy procession of boys and girls, calling out "good-night!" "good-boy!" at the top of their voices, down to where the Waterbaby was lying. All round the quays a still larger crowd of old women, sailors, babies, and idlers was assembled to watch us depart. Their excitement became quite ridiculous when we stepped like ordinary mortals into the boat and pulled slowly away, bowing right and left to the fat jolly old fish-wives, who were waving their handkerchiefs and curtseying with all their might. As only the two fishermen saw the Widgeon at all, for she lay quite out of sight behind the trees, I fancy the crowd believed we had come all the way from England in the Waterbaby, and that was partly the secret of our popularity.*

---

* Since this chapter was written, I have read M. Havard's interest-ing work, entitled the "Dead Cities of Zuyder Zee," from which it appears that he had visited Enkhuisen during his voyage in the previous year, 1873. A slight contretemps occurred to him at this place through the riotous conduct of some dyke-labourers. Perhaps the kindliness manifested towards the crew of the Waterbaby was due in part to a reaction of feeling. By the way, M. Havard, although evidently not much of a sailor, made his cruise in the Zuyder Zee in one of the country schuyts, fitted up for that purpose—a capital idea.

It was quite dark before we got on board again, and the yacht was only to be found by the glimmer of light in her cabin windows. The anchorage was quite silent and undisturbed.

CHAPTER XVII.

ENKHUISEN TO HARLINGEN.

THE Mate still peacefully slept while we others tripped the anchor, and the Widgeon stole away under all plain sail. When he woke up it was nearly ten o'clock, and he found himself completely out of soundings, figuratively speaking—like the individual in the "Arabian Nights," who went to sleep at Bagdad and opened his eyes again in Balsora.

There was a very light wind, N ½ W, with mist, and a little rain at intervals. The tide was hard against us, and we rather lost than gained in two or three long tacks across the Greupel Shoal. At last, however, the turning point was reached, and with a little harder breeze, after nearing Stavoren, we made effectual progress along the Friesland shore, which appeared rather prettily wooded about the vicinity of that historical hamlet. Near Hindeloopen, a small town conspicuous by its high church tower, it reassumes the usual common-place character. Thence, as far as one can see, all is level green dyke, varied only by dark timber groins running out at right angles into the sea.

Fortunately a good strong sailing breeze arose about noon, which obliged us to hand the big topsail, and, blowing right in our teeth, knocked up the sea into a lively commotion, which did a good deal to dispel the tedious dulness of our particularly slow progression. Two or three miles ahead, a large schuyt was pounding gallantly along, bruising the waves into white foam with her round bow, and scattering the spray aloft with the careless gaiety of a fine staunch new vessel. She ran faster through the water than we could, but the Widgeon seemed more weatherly. Still the gain we made was almost imperceptible. Tack and tack we kept together, and as there was really nothing else to speculate upon, the race created a little fund of excitement. It was well on in the afternoon when each craft, staying at the same moment, filled on opposite tacks, and we had the pleasare of showing our low lee bulwarks to our sturdy antagonist, as we crossed his bows. Two rugged-featured old seamen on board had a very long stare at the foreigners, in evident surprise at the little Widgeon's feat.

By this time the adverse tide was very weak, and we sailed close to an insignificant village called Makkum. The curious termination "um," by the way, is to be found in the names of towns in many parts of Groningen and Friesland, but seldom in the other Dutch provinces. A little south of "Makkum" is "Workum" (the conjunction suggests "Pigeon English" vagaries), then there are also "Akkrum," "Wirdum," "Kollum," and "Deinum," besides another place with the attractive title of "Winsum," and a couple of portentously-named islands off the coast, "Borkum" and "Rottum."

The general want of occupation awoke in the Mate and the Passenger, who had been smoking all the morning, a desire for improving literary pursuits, and they fished up out of a drawer an old book of dialogues for travellers, in four languages : unluckily Dutch was not one of them. This volume proved quite a mine of humour. Who could tire of listening to such conceits as these :

" *On a Lady's Toilette.*

" Clean that looking-glass a little ; it is quite dull. I look very ill this morning ; I did not sleep well last night ! "

" On the contrary, Madam, your complexion is very good, and your eyes are quite lively."

Space forbids inserting the variations on this theme in foreign tongues. What a useful book it was! Here come the maritime lucubrations of the illustrious unknown :

" *On Embarking, and of what happens at Sea.*

" I think the sea is very rough. The vessel is a great way out, and if a gale of wind came on, the boat might upset before we could reach her" . . .

" The wind increases! See that great wave which is coming to break against our vessel! I fear we shall have a storm! The sky is very dark towards the west!"

Then there is a pause, followed evidently by a crisis, which is thus unobtrusively alluded to :—

" The smell of the tar affects me!" . . .

"I am very much inclined to vomit!"!!! . . .

Arrived on shore, the unknown is dubious concerning the character of the bed linen; but a model innkeeper soothes him thus :—

" Do not be afraid, gentlemen; in our house the same sheets are never given to two persons!"

O fortunate nimium!

The mass of shoals which infest the northern portion of the Zuyder Zee, is bewildering to contemplate. Here, there, and everywhere, between Hindeloopen,

the Texel, Ter Schelling and the islands beyond, lies
at low tide, a desolate country of smooth wet mud
or sand, varied with patches of shallow water studded
with big buoys, like the ponds at the Crystal Palace
with fossil monsters. It was necessary to count
these individuals with the greatest care, in order to
make sure of our position on the chart, as we sailed
up the narrow channel of the Middel Gronden. A
few yards too far, on either side, as we tacked forwards and backwards, with just easy room to work in,
and no more, would have landed us high and dry on
a lurking sand-bank: no desirable situation. The
depth of water in this channel is four or five fathoms;
but when we crossed the lower end of the Kornwerder
shoal, the keel stirred up sand from the bottom, and
matters hardly improved in the Boompjes. This
latter approach to Harlingen, between the mainland
shore and a stretch of shoal ground entitled Het
Lange Zand, carries barely six feet along its whole
length from end to end, except in one spot, where the
lead sinks to four fathoms. Hescroff went forward
and conned, while I steered. Once we grounded
slightly, but scraped over without stopping, and many
were the narrow escapes.

Every minute would recur the cry of "Ready
about!" when down went the helm, round flew the
Widgeon into the wind's eye, her sails and spars

L

rattling and shaking, as for an instant she became upright. Then a warning shout of "heads!" and with a bouncing thump the main-boom would swing over, the Mate or the unwary Passenger barely escaping by a hair's-breadth from being knocked on the head. Then thirty seconds or so, "full and bye" on the other tack, speedily interrupted by the appearance of some striped and lettered buoy, like a Jack-in-the-box, right under our bowsprit. "Ready about!" again sings out the skipper, and about we go again, repeating the performance, with little variation, every half-minute, for an hour or more. Luckily the tide turned in our favour towards evening, helping us along at a fast walking pace, dead against the wind. At dusk the roofs of Harlingen loomed up ahead, and the Widgeon dashed between the piers very shortly afterwards. A crowd of men seized hold of the rope we flung from her bows, and towed her through the gates of the inner harbour, where we brought up abreast of a good quay.

It was quite dark by the time the Widgeon was comfortably settled in her berth. The "Heerenlogement," kept by De Haan, provided us with dinner, the first object of our solicitude. There was not much choice among the resources of the establishment, but at last some beefsteak, fruit, and cheese were set on the table by a naïve-looking girl, rather

timid at having to wait upon such unexpected
strangers. At dessert, the host, remarking our interest in a quaint old baptismal silver spoon, brought
out of a carved wooden cabinet quite a collection of
his family treasures. Many of the spoons bore dates
within the last ten years, but even these were nearly
all roughly worked with figures of Apostles on the
handles, exactly in the style of two centuries ago.

After Mr. de Haan's heirlooms had been duly
admired, the question was mooted whether we should
sleep at the hotel or not, but opinion swayed in
favour of the Widgeon's cabin. On returning thither
across one of the numerous bridges that cross the
little harbour, we became as usual unpleasantly aware
that it was not altogether inodorous.

CHAPTER XVIII.

HARLINGEN TO LEEUWARDEN.

A toilette levée—Robles de Billy—The " Hollandia "—Bric-à-brac
—" Condensed milk "—A present—The " lions " of Harlingen—
" Haul op de boom "—Franeker—Eise Eisinga—Collision—
" Nine-elms."

RISING late on Thursday, directly we put our
heads out of the cabin doors, whilst dressing in the
morning, we were met by a steady gaze from a group
of sight-seers on the quay above. One fat little
urchin I particularly noticed, standing with legs apart
and both hands in his baggy trousers-pockets, his
eyes fixed in a phlegmatic stare, and puffing away
placidly at a big china pipe, completely black from
age. This youthful smoker had weathered the storms
of perhaps eleven winters, perhaps less.

After breakfast came a walk over the town, which
is decidedly commonplace, but may pride itself, by
way of church, on one of the ugliest buildings in the
world. The massive dyke was erected after a disastrous inundation in 1566, by the Spanish governor,
Robles de Billy, in a manner at that time novel. To
their grateful ancestors, who set up a stone statue

of the worthy hidalgo, the present inhabitants are indebted for their only other monument. Harlingen in all probability, sank once as low as Enkhuizen, but is now the seat of a lively trade with England in cattle, cheese, and butter. Nearly all the surplus produce of the rich agricultural provinces adjoining passes through this insignificant port, enriching its ten thousand seafaring people on the way. Steamers ply to Hull and London. One of them, the " Hollandia," was lying in the harbour at the time of our visit. Hescroff made the acquaintance of her mate, who gave us the first English newspaper we had seen since leaving Ostend. The captain, moreover, kindly spared us a few bucketfuls of water, that liquid being less plentiful at Harlingen than schiedam, and very much more unwholesome.

Nearly all the women here wear upon their foreheads the curious convex gilt or golden plates, which we had seen worn by the old Fries lady in the Paleis garden at Amsterdam. Their effect is very rich and quaint, when they glisten against white caps and ruddy faces, in the full rays of the sun. Little jeweller's windows in every street are full of them, at all prices, from about fifteen shillings to as many pounds. The Passenger, who had acquired quite an appetite for silver trinkets, must needs wander from shop to shop in search of antique novelties. We succeeded admir-

ably in explaining ourselves by words and signs, and
soon found the dialect much more like English than
in other parts of Holland.   Scarcely any relics of the
past were to be unearthed among the jewellers, but
the Passenger did buy for less than a sovereign, the
neatest of tiny polished wooden trays, with a Lilli-
putian breakfast service of sixteen pieces, exquisitely
fashioned in silver.   In compensation for the scarcity
of old work, all the modern ornaments in the shops,
especially the silver cigarette holders, and filagree
brooches, were not without a flavour of antiquity.   The
patterns had seen no change for a century at least,
and the cheapness of the labour was not a little surprising.   For twenty pence I bought a pair of earrings,
quite elaborately wrought in almost a shilling's weight
of silver.

On returning to the Widgeon, a council of war took
place about our future routes, when we suddenly discovered the want of a chart for the Elbe river, rather
a discomposing dilemma, which was only at last got
over by purchasing one from the Hollandia, which
had formerly plied to Hamburg.   Finally, it was decided to go by canal to Leeuwarden, whence we
hoped to reach Groningen by the same inland progression, purposing afterwards to enter the German
Ocean through the Dollart estuary of the Ems.

Accordingly, in the afternoon, like a prudent ship-

owner, I repaired to a provision store to lay in a stock
of biscuit, cocoa, schiedam, preserved milk, and meat.
The proprietor spoke broken English, and his first
words, after a long and tedious exordium on my part,
were, "You want sell condensded milk, what you
price?" This took me rather aback, but after much pa-
tient explanation, during the course of which his face
lightened up considerably, on comprehending that my
business was buying, not selling; he showed the way
into a kind of loft, where hams, pickled beef, rope,
ship-biscuit, and hardware lay jumbled up together.
It took me at least two hours to make the necessary
purchases, in the midst of which, when the worthy
storekeeper discovered that my "plaisir schuyt" was
no ordinary vessel of burden, he promptly introduced
me to his "vrouw" and to a couple of Dutch skippers,
with whom, of course, it was *de rigueur* to wet the
occasion in schiedam.

A wheel-barrowful of bread, fresh from the baker's
oven, completed our victualling. On returning at sunset I sculled the Waterbaby down the harbour, and
was followed by a crowd of people, attracted by the
spectacle of the strange little boat. At night, my
friend the storekeeper came down to look at the
Widgeon, and in the fulness of his heart, when he left,
presented me with a parcel of about two dozen cigars,
wrapped up in brown paper.

By this time, beyond all question, we were the "lions" of Harlingen, and on Friday morning, held a very animated levée on the quay, during our matutinal toilette, with much the same feelings as those with which, I imagine, the noble animals in the Zoological gardens regard their human visitors. Intense, almost parental interest was displayed in such trivial details of our ablutions, as the public eye could catch, but the greatest excitement was caused by a report that we cooked provisions without fire!

As far as I could make out by questioning people, the arrival of an English yacht was a novelty unparalleled in the history of the port, and so we were made a great deal more of here than even in the canals between Rotterdam and Amsterdam, where a few pass every summer.

The seafaring folks all expressed astonishment at our having successfully crossed the Zuyder Zee without a pilot, and I really think their voyages must be very local, for they spoke of the capital as if it were as far away as Timbuctoo.

The forenoon was consumed in negotiations for a horse and man to tow us to Leeuwarden, a distance of about seventeen miles. At half past one, we started from our berth, and passed through several bridges into a lock, where there was a delay of many minutes. While there, M. Harmers, the English consul, very kindly introduced himself, and gave me a letter to his friend M. de Kempenaer, who resided at the place of our destination.

On the opening of the lock, the horse took the Widgeon rapidly in tow, along a winding narrow canal, with depth of water for her in the middle only. Its banks are very low, and over them the flat fertile country may be seen stretching away for miles, seamed with watercourses, and dotted with pretty villages. Close to the town are a number of large and very picturesque limekilns, built of bricks alternating with huge baulks of timber laid horizontally, their ends protruding at the sides.

The weather as usual was beautifully fine, though a fine fresh breeze was carrying along the laden schuyts that met us, at a rattling pace. The smooth water rippled and crackled under their bows as they surged on, their great booms brushing the long grass on the banks of the canal, in which, from its narrowness, there was often a difficulty in passing them. The Widgeon actually did ground once from this cause, and would have done so oftener, had not their crews treated us with much courtesy, invariably moving their booms amidships, to give us more room.

"Haul op de boom," we used to cry out, when we saw one sweeping along, and whatever language our adjuration is couched in, the worthy Dutchmen comprehended the situation at once, and always complied.

In the middle of the afternoon we came to a town, the name of which I could not make out, where a remarkably sharp corner, less than a right angle, taxed our watermanship to get safely round. The helm had to be put hard a-starboard, and the horse awakened into a trot, to escape going ashore.

Towards five o'clock, the quaint old-world village of Franeker hove in sight. We nearly ran into the draw-bridge, that was rather tardily opened, in spite of a stentorian hail from the Mate. A crowd of inhabitants inspected us, while the horse was having a feed of corn, and I sketched some caricatures of small boys coming home from school, which caused great fun. It was ludicrous to see the little scamps quarrelling for the coppers we flung amongst them.

This ancient place was once the seat of an important university—but now the times are changed. There is to be seen in a private house a curious astronomical model, very much the same thing as an orrery, which imitates the motions of the heavenly bodies in a most undisguisedly material way. Eise Eisinga was the not uneuphonious name of the burgher who constructed it, about the year of our Lord 1780.

The sun was inclining down to the horizon behind our backs as we left Franeker, and began to meet

schuyt after schuyt crowded with country people
returning from a grand fair at Leeuwarden, of which
we had heard rumours in Harlingen. Several of
them were passing the uplifted bridge of one large
nameless village as we approached, and as there
seemed plenty of room to go by, we did not slack
the tow-rope, intending to shoot through with the
momentum we retained. What was our horror to see
the nearest schuyt steering directly at us! All was
over, I thought, except the shouting, when with a
mutual speed of six or eight miles an hour, the two
craft ran into one another stem on!

Up the Dutchman's slanting bulwarks rushed our
bowsprit, bending like a strung bow, and into the
centre of a large watercask on his forecastle deck,
upon which a young fellow had seated himself at the
last moment, with the idea of lessening the force of
the collision. It sent him flying, however, barrel and
all, while the Widgeon was lifted several inches out
of water forward, never stopping till her bobstay
tackle caught the Dutchman's stem; after this she
gradually slid backwards, wonderful to relate, without
any injury. A volley of epithets, which, as they were
not understood, fell perfectly harmless, passed between the two craft, as they gathered way and glided
past. The danger seemed over, when a second schuyt,
with only a couple of men on board, came into colli-

sion with our starboard quarter, and immediately afterwards a third, steered by a one-eyed old man, made straight for us, this time apparently of pure malice prepense. However, the Passenger seized a boat-hook and pushed the schuyt, which was light in ballast, out of our way ashore. The old man brandished an oar, and scowled with such an expression of rage, that we all thought he was going to "run a muck" at us. Some of the villagers picked up stones, but their resolution hung fire; one by one they dropped their extemporised weapons, the Widgeon glided on, and the opportunity for what seemed likely to prove a serious affray passed, very luckily for all concerned.

Nothing could excuse the conduct of the schuyts, but it may perhaps be partly explained by the fact of the men being half-drunk, and dazed with the bright setting sun in their eyes. It is also just possible that we may have unconsciously broken some rule of the road. All the other craft we met behaved well as usual, though crowded with excited country people coming home from the fair.

At twilight, in a picturesque reach of the canal, we passed a pretty village among thick trees, the name of which, as I took it down in my notes from our driver's word of mouth, was "Nine-elms." Rather surprised at meeting with such an old acquaintance

so far afield, a few days afterwards I referred to a
Dutch map, which, as I almost expected, knew it not,
but indicated our village by a round black dot under
the eccentric name of " Deinum." If all my attempts
at phonetic spelling are as little to be relied on as
this one, they evidently would not prove of much
assistance to future travellers. Deinum church
attracted attention by its red brick tower, surmounted by a cupola, with a peculiar slated dome.

A mile or two further of quiet travelling in the
dusk, along a still canal, with banks embowered in
trees, brought us to the outskirts of Leeuwarden,
where our driver was paid off, and we took up a
berth for the night among a number of small craft.
It was too late, after supper, to go into the town, but
we smoked the nocturnal cigar close by our floating
home, in a deep-shadowed lonely place, fringed with
lofty trees, where the sound of music and revelry was
wafted at intervals from the noisy public squares.
The Passenger, imbued with the poetry of the scene,
burst into a flood of conversation, which whiled away
the time so fast, that it was midnight before we retired
to rest, and the consequence was a general disinclina-
tion to rise next morning.

CHAPTER XIX.

LEEUWARDEN.

The " Kermis " — Prinsentuin — Old china — Café-chantant — The Widgeon a "stoom-boot" — Dutch play — Leaning towers — Fries proverb — The circus — Story of Cinderella — Change of plans.

TWO unwelcome discoveries were made on Saturday morning at breakfast: one, that our magnificent Harlingen ham was rotten at the core; the other, that we had scarcely any ready money left. This necessitated waiting until a remittance could arrive from Brunsbüttel, for the Leeuwarden Bank has no correspondence with England.

In the course of the morning we called on M. de Kempenaer, who received us with the utmost kindness, and went with us to a concert in the Prinsentuin, a pretty little public garden which was formerly attached to the royal palace.

After the music was over, the "kermis," or fair, was to be visited. All Friesland seemed collected together in the great squares of its capital, which were occupied for the time by long avenues of open booths. The commodities in the ascendant were toys, cakes, fancy wares and articles of feminine attire, but at least a couple of the larger booths displayed old china for sale. Enthusiastic collectors in Leeuwarden are passionately fond of " blue oriental." This mania seems quite in accord with the traditional Dutch taste for bright contrasts of colour, as exemplified in the old tulip " craze." Leaving the china shop, a few steps brought us to a large open space, in one of the outskirts of the town, full of painted canvas erections, which after nightfall, were illuminated with glaring gas jets, above the heads of a surging crowd. Among them were shooting galleries, theatres, peepshows, café-chantants, merry-go-rounds, manageries, and, to crown all, a great circus, the like of which Leeuwarden had never seen before. Reserving a visit to the latter for Monday, and passing by several " cosmoramas," and an exhibition of automatons, which advertised in large letters, " een mekanische Goochelaar, Drinker, Snoeper, Rooker, en Menscheneter " (what can a " Snoeper " be ?) we entered a café-chantant.

This place of entertainment was kept by a Frenchman, and although only a temporary concern, was well fitted with tables and chairs, and included English bottled beer in its list of refreshments. On a sort of daïs at one side of the room, seven painted ladies were seated, under the supervision of a matronly old duenna, at whose nod they alternately sang French and German songs. Presently they retired, and the stage was occupied by the conventional negro minstrel of the London streets. He sang one of the well-known melodies of St. James's Hall, and then began a perfectly pointless dialogue with his wife, which, although quite incomprehensible to the audience, was, nevertheless, received with tumultuous applause. In fact, the odd thing was that not one performance, during the whole evening, was given in Dutch.

A bright starlit night heralded a very hot Sunday morning. Our thermometer stood at 96 degrees Fahrenheit in the shade, inside the cabin, when M. de Kempenaer came down to pay a call, and found us in the coolest of attire. A crowd of holiday-makers was hardly ever absent from the bank over-looking our decks. We could hear them remark in Fries upon every peculiarity that struck them. One prevailing idea seemed to be, that the "Widgeon" was a "stoom-boot"; no doubt, because the only sharp-bowed vessels in Holland are the little canal steamers.

Very little favour was accorded to the story that we came from England. Some one suggested that we might possibly have come on the deck of a larger vessel, and I think this latter theory was eventually adopted. Our invisible cookery again attracted considerable speculation and curiosity, but the awning veiled the reality from the sharpest eyes.

Entering the town at night, we witnessed the serious tragedy of "de Komponist en de Orgelman," very well acted in Dutch, although the theatre was nothing but one of the large booths erected for the week of the kermis.

Bright sunny weather prevailed again on Monday. The windless heat quite overcame the Mate and the Passenger, so I went out alone with M. de Kempénaer who had kindly offered to show me the antiquities of Leeuwarden.

These are but few, if we except some picturesque middle-aged houses of the ordinary Dutch character. One of the church towers is however very remarkable. The lower portion leans two or three feet out of the perpendicular, the result of a subsidence which evidently occurred while it was being built. The architect, however, carried out his contract by erecting a spire on the top, inclined as much in the opposite direction! The effect is very ludicrous.

Holland is emphatically the country of leaning towers. Any heavy building must, in that swampy soil, be constructed upon a bed of piles driven closely together, and where possible, down to a firm bottom. If by any chance the weight of the superstructure

M

displaces any of the piles, the tower leans over in consequence, like a carriage on a weak spring.

The splendid Gothic belfry, all that remains of the abbey-church, or cathedral of Leeuwarden, exhibits what sailors call a "heavy list," from the subsidence of its foundation almost five feet down. The extent of the consequent inclination from the perpendicular is difficult to ascertain, as the depression is deeper at one corner than at any of the other three, and matters are further complicated by a crack, passing through the crowns of the window arches, from top to bottom of the stately edifice.

The ascent is made by a dark and rugged stone winding staircase, in mounting which a stranger is thrown against the wall, every time the spiral dips in its revolutions, towards the sunken angle. In an old account of a visit to the leaning tower of Pisa, the same peculiarity is recorded of the staircase leading up to the summit of that famous curiosity. After several repetitions of this experience we reached a large loft, in which was to be seen a mass of ancient clockwork and two enormous bells, the larger of which would have held me standing upright, and weighs—heaven only knows how many thousand pounds. One story higher still I climbed, and was amply rewarded for my trouble. The view was magnificent. Mile upon mile, at my feet, stretching away into the dim blue distance, lay rich meadows and waving cornfields, intersected with winding streaks of canal and river, and dotted with dark luxuriant groves, red roofs, tall spires, domes, vessels, windmills, and cattle. All was the conquest of man—stolen from the sleepless sea! The province of Friesland, since the year A.D. 533, has been inundated in a disastrous manner no less than thirty-four times! On some of these occasions hundreds of square miles were submerged, and thousands of industrious peasants drowned amongst the ruins of their villages.

The old belfry tower, from which the scene of so many disasters can be surveyed, is tottering to its fall, now that a safe and fertile country, for the first time in history, looks up to it with careless unconcern. The people of Leeuwarden attempt no repair, although the hoary giant deserves a better fate. Unfortunately, I fear the ravages of neglect have spread too far, and that nothing now can save it. Ruin, when it comes, will be sudden and complete. So toughly the materials, hard red brick and grey stone, adhere together, that nothing short of the collapse of one entire half, the inevitable result of a little further subsidence, can wreak its complete dissolution. Then every fragment will doubtless be carried away, as the ruined nave has been, to serve in building houses for generations yet unborn.

Dinner-time interrupted the current of my regrets, and descending the winding stair more readily than I mounted it, I repaired to the Widgeon, where the Mate and the Passenger awaited me.

We were invited to dine with M. de Kempenaer, and were afterwards to pay our long deferred visit to the circus. At dessert the conversation turned on the similitude of the Fries language to English, and our host quoted a common saying in the province, which being interpreted runs thus—

> "Who cannot say '*bread*,' '*butter*,' '*cheese*,'
> That man is not good Fries."

pronouncing the words in italics exactly as we do.

The entertainment at the circus in the evening was very amusing. Tumbling and conjuring was the prelude to a representation by children of the story of Cinderella, in dumb show. People had been sent on, a month before the fair, to select and train children of the town to bear the minor parts, the character of the prince being taken by a little golden-haired boy of six, who was already quite an accomplished gymnast, and his elder sister, of about thirteen, acted with precocious *savoir faire* as mistress of the ceremonies at his tiny court.

First of all Cinderella, a small girl, dressed in a dirty ragged old shawl, is discovered up to the neck in household work. Then enter the two naughty sisters, each barely three feet high, attired for the ball in magnificent court costume. They strut before a tall pier glass, admire themselves, laugh, and slap the cheeks of poor little Cinderella. A gilded carriage, hardly larger than a bath chair, and drawn by a pair of ponies no bigger than mastiff dogs, is driven up to them by a boy coachman, bewigged and bepowdered in the most imposing fashion. They step in and clatter away, leaving their sister wringing her tiny hands in despair. But the conventional old grandmother fairy, with the fearfullest of features, the tallest of tall hats, and the gayest of scarlet cloaks, bounces in, magic wand in hand. All the transformations follow in due course, and like a radiant princess, Cinderella rides off in the quondam pumpkin, beaming with contented smiles.

Then there comes a pause. Men in uniform dash into the arena, bearing tall candlesticks and ballroom furniture, which they arrange in a wonderfully short space of time, and we are transported at once into the company of his royal highness the prince. One after another the guests arrive, these naughty sisters among the first, and range themselves in couples for a dance. The little mites of children are dressed up in caricature of the great characters on the political stage of the day. There is Bismarck, booted, spurred, and helmeted like a lifeguardsman. Kaiser Wilhelm wags his white whiskers at the supreme altitude of three feet six inches from the ground. Sad and dejected enters a miniature copy of Napoleon, arm in arm with the quaintest little facsimile of M. Thiers, a gravely toddling urchin of barely three years old. Many others follow; last but not least in the estimation of the audience, General Van Swieten, the hero of the hour, fresh from his Atchinese campaign, who is greeted with deafening cheers.

Cinderella comes late; but when she enters all fall aside, astonished at her beauty and magnificence. The prince descends from his throne to lead off the dance with her, and a pretty concerted ballet is gone through, while M. Thiers, pettishly refusing to speak to Bismarck, sulks in a corner with his imperial master. So the old nursery tale is carried out, until everybody is reconciled to everybody, and Cinderella marries the prince. Then, with a flourish of trumpets in roll a dozen little carriages, each drawn by the most exiguous of ponies, the children rush into them, wild with delight, amidst a thunder of applause, and are driven three times round and round. At last they all disappear through a side-door, and the performance is at an end.

On our return to the Widgeon a consultation was held, which resulted in a change of plans. M. Harmers had assured us, when we left Harlingen, that it was extremely doubtful whether the depth of the country canals would permit our ship to reach Groningen; and as this was confirmed by M. de Kempenaer, it was resolved to give up the attempt. In lieu therefore of reaching the German Ocean by the Dollart and the river Ems, we now decided to enter it at a nearer point, the Lauwer Zee, passing by canal through Dokkum. The Passenger, not caring to visit Brunsbüttel, resolved to leave us for a few days, to fall in with us again at Hamburg.

CHAPTER XX.

LEEUWARDEN TO DOKKUM AND THE LAUWER ZEE.

Waterbirds—Dokkum—Irish flax merchants—The "shibboom"—Dokkumer Siehl—"Zeven uur"—Aground ! and off again !—Englishman's Flat—Schiermonnik Island—A thunderstorm—A dilemma—Gutturals—The "dumb persuasion"—Ostmahorn.

AT last, on Tuesday morning, came the long-expected remittance from Germany, with an explanation of the delay, which was caused by the remissness of the postal authorities at Leer, a town on the frontier. Paying a farewell visit to M. de Kempenaer, seeing the Passenger off to the railway station, and provisioning the Widgeon in a great hurry, we started late in the afternoon, towed by a couple of sturdy boys along the town canal, to a spot where a man had been ordered to be ready for us with a horse. Many houses and beautiful trees look down upon its winding waters here, but, not far beyond, the canal loses its picturesque character. The horse took us in tow at about half-past five, and we reached Dokkum between nine and ten o'clock at night, after a journey of about thirteen miles, not interrupted by any striking incident. The country appeared rich and fertile, and there were a surprising

number of storks and waterbirds feeding tamely by
the side of our route.

It would have been rather a puzzle to find out
where to go in the dark, after dismissing the driver,
had we not, by a lucky chance, happened to bring up
almost opposite the cottage door of a labourer who
spoke a little English, having been a seaman in the
American Navy. He came out, attracted by the
noise, just after I had jumped ashore over a schuyt,
the occupants of which came stumbling out of bed
shivering on deck in the night air, venting many loud
objurgations against me for disturbing their peaceful
slumbers. Our new friend set everything to rights
by a word or two, and then good-naturedly accompanied us to several shops, interpreting our wants.
The landlord of the principal hotel, where we filled
up our store of beer (who is also the owner of a very
neat little screw-steamer, which plies to Harlingen
and Leeuwarden), spoke our language quite fluently ;
he assured me that he had gleaned his knowledge
solely from the Irish flax-merchants, who annually
visit the town to make purchases in their trade.
What a curious ramification of commerce in this
obscure locality !

Returning to the Widgeon laden with provender
of all kinds, our interpreter was ludicrously struck
with the length of her bowsprit, which could be

dimly made out by the flickering light of the anchor-lamp. "O Chris', what for a shibboom!"* he cried out, and the sight so pleased him that he must needs introduce us to his wife and his cottage. The latter was clean, and neatly, though scantily, furnished with dark wooden chairs and presses. Coarse blue delft ware, bright-polished brass candlesticks and utensils competed by way of ornament with gaudy lithographs of American frigates, with all their yards manned and all their guns belching flame at once. It was easy to see that the poor man's affection was divided between his old service and his homely vrouw, who was quite in keeping with her surroundings. In broken English he explained, "I work on de canal for de vrouw, but my heart it is always on de sea." After this touching sentiment we gave him a small present and left, as it was getting very late, having first engaged a horse and driver for the next day.

The night was rough and dark, but the morning broke very fine, although there were signs of hard weather out at sea, in the white fleecy clouds blown rapidly over the sky. We rose late, and waited a long time for the promised means of locomotion, which did not appear to be forthcoming. However, the landlord of the hotel kindly paid us a visit about

* A jibboom.

noon, and explained that the horse was probably ready, but on the other side of the town, where the towpath begins. Accordingly we tied a couple of reefs in the mainsail and were off in a trice, tearing the water at a rapid pace, under the old earthwork fortifications, covered with trees and red-roofed houses. A crowd of people followed running along the ramparts, cheering, as the Widgeon with the bit between her teeth, rushed round the difficult corners in brilliant style. We shot the bridge at such a rate that its guardian was not ready with his pole and bag, and looked at our retreating figures with a most rueful expression of countenance. However, I signalled him to pursue in his boat, which he did, and caught his fee wrapped up in a piece of paper, when we hauled down the mainsail, and moved along more leisurely under foresail alone.

Sure enough, when we reached the other side of the town, there stood a huge grey horse awaiting us, looking the picture of patience, and as if he had been a fixture there for a century at least. It was half-past one when the tow-line was rigged, and with the strong wind aft he made no more of us than a feather, breaking every now and then into a lively jog-trot. The canal was narrow and winding, but rather deep, and we only met three schuyts on our way. On either side little was to be seen but thick fields of wheat and barley hanging in fringes of heavy ears over the tow-path. Eight miles were got over at such a pace, that by three o'clock our destination, the tiny hamlet of Dokkumer Siehl, was reached, and we came to a full stop in front of a lock, which divided us from the waters of the Lauwer Zee.

An air of calm repose pervaded the place. The landscape was made up of acre on acre of yellow cornfields and wet green pasture, with mile upon mile of muddy flats, bounded by a silvery line of sea in the distance, and where we stood, by a lofty dyke. The stillness grew unearthly when the wind dropped, and nothing broke silence but the cries of waterbirds busily searching for worms and shellfish on the mud. One by one the three native craft ranged up alongside, and their crews, pipe in mouth, set themselves calmly to wait for the opening of the lock. Slowly the sun sank lower in the sky, gilding their dark tanned features, while they discussed the result of certain culinary operations gone through by their burly vrouws. Although we tried very hard to make them understand our questions, it was all in vain. Only one piece of information could we get, but that was not unwelcome—that our release would come at " zeven uur." * They displayed an utter incurious stolidity, shaking their heads with mystified

* Seven o'clock.

looks, even when we displayed a chart, in the forlorn
hope of learning something about our route. At last
all attempt at conversation was given up in despair.
Slowly and gradually the tide arose, covering all the
mud flats up to the foot of the dyke, and punctually
at seven, without a word on either side, we were let
into and out of the lock.

The channel outside is extremely narrow, and even
at the top of the flood has a very small depth of
water, probably not more than eight feet at most.
It is marked out by perches, but only on the starboard hand. At half-ebb the mud uncovers, and
then the steep banks disclose its course beyond the
possibility of mistake. At the time when we began
leisurely setting sail, however, in the expectation of
being preceded by the schuyts, all distinctions were
obliterated by a sheet of water covering the flats, and
it was quite a disappointment to see the Dutch
mariners calmly settling themselves to rest for the
night where they were. Nevertheless, on we went,
the light failing wind and ebbing tide bearing us
along at a smart walking pace.

The last few inches of water were draining off the
mud, and already the gulls and tern were circling
about in flocks, in quest of their slimy nutriment.
One over-bold little fellow, giving Hescroff a capital
chance, was knocked over with the Belgian gun, and

secured by means of the Waterbaby. The boat was
hardly in tow again, before we sidled gently on to
the starboard bank; but it was only a passing graze.
Then came another good opportunity of hitting a
tern. I luffed the Widgeon a little to port;
Hescroff blazed away but missed, and the next
moment the well-known dull grating sound arose
from under the keel, and we were fast ashore on the
port side of the channel. About three quarters of a
mile only had been made good when this catastrophe
occurred, and it became at once clear to all of us,
that we should get no further that night. The force
of her impact had lifted the Widgeon some inches
out of water at the bows, by sliding up the slippery
steep incline of adhesive clay. To add to our troubles
a thunderstorm with heavy rain came on, and gave
us a thorough wetting while we stowed the sails, in
the midst of which occupation one of our late companions came rippling down before the breeze, her
crew all showing their teeth in a broad grin of
amusement. To our delight she too stuck fast a
little further on, but blundered off again just before
dusk, and we saw her no more.

After all, as Hescroff remarked, "We didn't need
to anchor, and we might have been worse off," with
which philosophical consolation he proceeded to
cook supper. In the twilight, when the tide had

fallen sufficiently, we were visited by two individuals
who had walked over the mud from Dokkumer Siehl,
on discovering our plight. One, a rough-looking seaman, speaking a few words of English, expressed
his intention of sailing with us as pilot, and upon his
company being respectfully declined, grew quite con-
temptuous and satirical. However, when I had
carefully explained to him that we selected our present berth on purpose, and were always in the habit
of choosing suitable mud banks to ground on for the
night, he became thoughtful, and decamped with his
mate.

After this we were left alone with our adventure.
Night closed in dull and gloomy, with no moon.
The wind soughed mournfully through the rigging,
ropes rattled, sea-birds plashed and cried, and far off
thunder growled in a low-pitched chorus without.
Inside the little cabin all was light and comfort, but I
could not help speculating on the difficulty of threading the channel next day, till at length sleep closed
my eyes. No watch was kept or required, for we
were in security from every danger, and had no expectation of getting afloat before daylight.

Three or four hours passed unconsciously on, but
about half-past two o'clock, a draught of cold air
awoke me with a slight feeling of misgiving. Without
at first rising, I seemed to feel the peculiar sensation

of being afloat, and when a heavy rain-squall struck
the yacht, she certainly heaved and rolled as nothing ever did high and dry upon a mud bank.
Jumping on deck in an instant I found the tide rising,
the flats all covered up, and our ship lightly touching
with her stern the opposite side of the channel to that
on which the grounding had taken place. Nothing
more could be made out through the atmosphere,
dark with a load of mist and rain. Even the perches
that mark the way, were all invisible except one,
which was almost in contact with the Widgeon. I
roused Hescroff, and we anchored her in mid
channel, then retired to rest again until the first grey
glimmer of dawn should peer above the horizon.

In an hour it had brightened sufficiently to disclose
the unpleasantness of the weather in its full extent.
A strong wind was blowing, and black-bellied rain
clouds rushed wildly overhead from the S.S.W., while
for summer time, the air was bitterly cold. In the
distance, by the lock, we could just espy five schuyts
hoisting their great white sails to be in readiness for
a start. This time we were determined the Dutchmen were to show us the way unasked, so just as
they came winging past us in Indian file, up went
our mainsail in a leisurely way, with tack aloft, and
as it was no part of our plan to overhaul our pilots
too quickly, the jib was left unset.

Nevertheless the hindmost of the squadron was very soon caught, greatly to the surprise of her crew, who gazed at us open-mouthed as we passed, and our sailing was so neatly timed, that we headed the foremost exactly when the channel got wider, and our difficulties were at an end. The latter part of it is marked with perches on both sides, as far as a white buoy to starboard, whence we took our departure, on a compass course about N. by E. through a broad passage between the Friesland shore, and a sand called the Ballast flat, protruding nearly three miles out from the province of Groningen. From a black buoy on the edge of the one fathom shoal off Ostmahorn, the course is N. W. to another off the ominously named Englishman's Flat, a bank of sand uncovered at low water, and marked by two beacons close together. A wide channel leads out N. by E. again, from hence into the German Ocean, in the midst of a maze of ever-changing shoals, over a bar with little more than six feet of water upon it. Every gale alters the depth of the water-ways and the disposition of the buoys, so that no chart is to be depended upon for two years running, and I strongly advise any yachtsman who attempts the passage, to charter a pilot from Ostmahorn.

With us all went merrily as a marriage bell, until off the Island of Schiermonnik. This little isolated patch of green-tipped, sandy dunes, had been visible for several hours before we reached it. On its western end, a pair of tall slender columnar light-houses tower a hundred and forty-seven and a hundred and thirty-nine feet, respectively, into the air, distinguishing it from others of the string of similar islands, which fringes the coast for a hundred miles. Gaily our little vessel dashed by its desolate shores, and already we were congratulating ourselves on having successfully picked up, one after another, most of the complicated buoys which mapped out our route, when a thunderstorm came on.

Now thunderstorms are picturesque, and enliven tame scenery, but they also have an unpleasant habit of bringing wind and sea in their train ; the very circumstances of all others, which we would have most gladly dispensed with at this particular moment.

A dense cloud, black as night, flew swiftly forwards, brooding low upon the water in a mist of driving hail. We prepared by lowering the main peak and clewing up the tack, for the impending squall, luffed as it burst in fury upon us with a shower of icy missiles, and then in a few seconds, after bowing down to the blast and staggering slowly on, the yacht recovered herself in a momentary calm. The storm passed harmlessly away, with one farewell clap of thunder, but a fresh breeze followed, which caused a lively commotion in the sea, obliterating all the shoals and channels in a turmoil of white-capped waves. What completed our discomfiture, however, was that in the excitement we had not only lost count of our position, but the buoys ahead seemed nearly twice as many as those marked upon the chart. Whether this was really the case, I cannot tell, but at any rate our confusion was very genuine. Half a mile ahead two good sized country craft were bouncing about in the white water, evidently by the short tacks they made avoiding some hidden danger, but nothing was to be gleaned from observation of their movements.

In this dilemma, we suddenly made out a fishing smack running down towards us before the wind, and hove-to in order to intercept her, and, if possible, procure a pilot. Meanwhile, as we had been astir so very betimes, the Mate, who prided himself on a certain delicacy in the manipulation of buttered eggs, set about preparing a second breakfast, in which that dainty was to play no inconsiderable part. Just as perfection seemed within his grasp—misfortunes never come single—the Widgeon gave one impatient plunge, and over went spirit lamp, dish and all, on the floor of the forecastle.

The smack was by this time close alongside, but I was obliged to board her in the Waterbaby, for she possessed no boat. Two rugged old fishermen were her sole occupants, and the flood of gutturals with which they greeted my essays at conversation, would have scared an etymologist. At last I pointed to my bark, and one of them seating himself like Charon at my side, we reached the Widgeon, and he took the helm. An interchange of ideas had been somehow achieved, but only to a very limited extent. He dimly comprehended that we wanted a pilot, and I gathered from his frequent mention of the words "Engelsch" and "Ostmahorn" that he intended to take us to some person in that village, who spoke our language, and, as the event proved, I was right.

The Widgeon made short tracks before the wind, which had veered in the thunder squall, back towards Ostmahorn. As for the smack which followed, although she measured fully fifteen tons, we left her easily astern. Our Palinurus was evidently delighted and astonished at what he considered wonderful speed, and a glass of schiedam rendered him still more talkative than before. Hescroff and he entered into a most animated discussion, of which half the sentences began or ended with "Johnny Piloto," but. for all one understood of the other, they might as well have been born dumb, and died, as Mrs. Malaprop says, "in that persuasion."

Ostmahorn, a little cluster of red-roofed cottages peeping over the top of a dyke, and boasting a wooden landing-jetty, was reached as early as ten o'clock in the morning, such good use had we made of our time, before being forced to retrace our steps.

Our adventures in this place must occupy another chapter.

CHAPTER XXI.

OSTMAHORN AND THE LAUWER ZEE, BY THE GERMAN OCEAN, TO BRUNSBÜTTEL ON THE ELBE.

Government pilots—Dutch skippers—Ladies on board—Schiermonnik Oog—Thunderclouds—A calm—The Ems river—Midnight watch — Sunrise — Juist — Hanover—Norderney—Beacons—Baltrum— Naiads—Porpoises—The log—Heligoland—The Elbe—Cuxhaven —Hills again !—Brunsbüttel.

UPON arriving at Ostmahorn, the anchor was dropped in about eight feet of water, the sails lightly furled, and then I went ashore with Hescroff, our pilot, and the beer barrel. The fisherman took us to the house of the Postmaster, a good-natured elderly man, who spoke very fair English, and whose only son had but just returned home from a situation in England. He explained to me that our guide's volubility merely signified, that for the modest sum of 500 gulden he would be content to pilot us to the Elbe, the way to which he may, presumably, have known, although even that is far from certain. The old gentleman's eye twinkled when I suggested that 500 gulden (about £40!!) appeared at first sight perhaps a little beyond the ordinary tariff, and that

we had better adjourn to the inn to talk the matter
over. His opinion seemed to be that the absurd demand was made because the man did not really want
to go. But there must have been a mistake some-
where, for when it was made clear to him that I could
scarcely accede to his terms, the rugged old son of the
sea fairly sat down and began to cry. The next
minute he was all gratitude and smiles, on receiving
the same fee as the government pilot would have had,
for navigating our craft in from the sea, that is to say,
about *eight shillings*.

Fortunately there was no need to employ him
again, as the village is a depôt for men licensed by
the Administration to pilot vessels of all nations,
who find themselves upon this difficult coast. These
men are thoroughly to be trusted, although their
wages are very low, not more than three shillings and
fourpence a day, but they expect of course, a gratuity
besides. On their caps they wear a little badge, and
should also be able to display a great brass medal,
about six inches across, the legend upon which I forget. The Postmaster drew up a form, which I signed,
and for which eight shillings and fourpence had to be
paid. This defrayed the wages of a pilot from
Ostmahorn to the sea, when, in case it should prove
impossible, or inconvenient, to land him, I might retain his services at the daily rate of three shillings and

fourpence, until an opportunity occurred of sending him back.

A grey-haired little middle-aged man was despatched to gather up his kit in readiness for an early departure, while I entertained the Postmaster and two Dutch merchant skippers. One of these was a very intelligent sort of man, speaking English very fairly. He knew the Solent well, and was loud in his praises of several well-known English yachts. After a good deal of conversation and still more beer and cigars, had become things of the hazy past, we adjourned to the Widgeon, and the pilot, whose kit was all contained in a blue cotton pocket handkerchief, came on board. A loud hail arrested us on the point of sailing off. It proceeded from a whole boatload of my Ostmahorn friends, with the addition of two ladies. Of course we stopped, and allowed them to inspect our little marine domicile, with which they were duly charmed, and left us with a shower of good wishes.

Shortly after noon we sped away with a fine breeze, hardly so strong as to necessitate the two reefs that were tied in the mainsail. However, a strong blast came down from a thunder-cloud off Schiermonnik Oog, and until three o'clock, when we shook out the reefs and set our topsail, the sky was full of hanging storms. Later in the afternoon it fell dead calm. A smooth oily swell was lifting and rolling our helpless

bark, and swaying her shivering sails to and fro, with
an irritating rattle. We were now four or five miles
outside Schiermonnik Oog, having made our exit an
hour or two earlier, with the greatest ease, by a totally
different channel from that which baffled our first
attempt. Since then the tide had changed, whereupon the seething white water disappeared entirely
in a smooth unruffled calm.

All the circumstances combined in suggesting one
only palliative of their discomfort, so I turned into
the cabin and snatched an hour's quiet slumber. On
awaking, the Widgeon seemed much further out at
sea, a light breeze had arisen from the south-south-
west, and we were steering about due east. A con-
tinuation of this course took us by six o'clock, some
distance within the fairway buoy of the river Ems,
whence the tall lighthouses of Schiermonnik Oog
were still plainly to be seen above the horizon astern.
Now another silent calm ensues, the stillness broken
only as before, by our clattering sails. The rolling
motion quite overcomes Hescroff, and makes me
wish myself anywhere else. The pilot steers; he
never seems happy without the helm in his hand.
He eats—he has an appetite! We look on despond-
ingly; we feel as if we should never eat again! In
three hours the progress of the Widgeon does not
amount to one mile. Shall we ever get away from

that hateful buoy, bobbing up and down, as if in mockery ?

Yes, at last that bank of dark threatening clouds, which has long been gathering in the west, nears us, creeping along the coast, and bringing with it a gentle sou'-sou'-westerly breeze. Dusk falls like a curtain over the sea. The dark smooth expanse is only relieved by the faint specks of flame in distant light-house towers, and by occasional flashes of thunderless lightning, that break the sombre intervolved cloud canopy. How small and insignificant we feel before this threatening parade of Nature's warlike force ! Still no storm falls ; the gentle breeze continues to waft us onwards : not even a drop of rain disturbs the air, and the little Widgeon wings her lonely way in peace. At last, about midnight, Hescroff relieves me of my watch and I turn exhausted to rest.

At sunrise, when I awoke, the impassive pilot stood like the "Ancient Mariner" at the helm, wet with the morning mist. A glass of schiedam revived him, and he was despatched into the forecastle to sleep. All night an E. ¾ S. course had been steered, in about nine fathoms of water, outside all the shoals and banks. Our progress had been considerable: we were abreast the island of Juist, off the coast of Hanover, and had sighted Norderney, conspicuous by its curious beacon, 134 feet in height. The only way in which many of these islands could be distinguished from one another at all is by means of erections of this character, with etched facsimiles of which the lower corner of our chart was profusely adorned. Some of the islands are frequented by the Germans in the summer for sea-bathing, but from the sea they hardly exhibit any trace of human habitation.

Not a cloud was in the sky when, with a fine light breeze, we passed Baltrum, at about half-past nine in the morning, and set the topsail and mizen, which had been prudently taken in at nightfall. Some miles astern a thunderstorm was raging, with frequent lightning and heavy rains; but it gradually sheered inland. Towards noon the weather became delightful; so clear the sky, so pure the emerald green sea, under the gentle wind and warm light of the sun.

> " What are flying hours to me,
> Tasting of eternity?
> What is wakeful care to me,
> Sailing an unfathomed sea?
> Let me lie and let me ponder,
> Careless where my bark may wander;
> Let the ever-rolling ocean
> Rock me with incessant motion,
> And the Zephyr breathe a song
> Aeolian, my path along,
> And the sunbeam ever shine
> O'er the ripple's dark blue line,

Underneath a sky serene,
Where no cloud was ever seen,
Lighting up the hollow main
Till all mysteries are plain,
Which the foamy caverns hide
Of the unrevealing tide ! "

So sang the Naiads ; but, alack-a-day ! there are no Naiads in the German Ocean—only porpoises. Am I dreaming, or have I drifted into poetry ? Let us turn to the prosaic log forthwith :—

" 1.25 p.m. Beacons at Lange Oog bear S.S.W., distant 4 miles.

1.30 „ Breeze veers to E.S.E., and strengthens, obliging us to closehaul, and dowse topsail.

3. 0 „ Calm.

4.25 „ Sounding shows 13 fathoms. Semaphore on Wange Oog bears S., nearly. Course E. for Elbe outer light-vessel, about 20 miles. Signed a paper stating that I had been unable to land the pilot. Hove patent log overboard.

5.25 „ Log shows three quarters of a mile. Tide with us. Beacons at mouth of Jahde River visible. Light airs from W. dead aft.

6.25 „ Log shows 7 furlongs for the hour.

7.25 „   „   1½ miles   „

Sighted Heligoland, distant about 14 miles.

8. 0 p.m. Dined—Indian curried fowl. Found three pounds of beef gone bad—threw it overboard.

8.15 „ Breeze from W.S.W.

8.25 „ Log shows 2½ miles for the hour.

·9.25 „ Hauled in log, showing 4¾ miles for the hour.

Passed Schlüssel (Key) buoy."

And so on.

The pilot's wakefulness, phlegm, and taciturnity were wonderful. He scarcely left the helm all this day, and never uttered a syllable without being spoken to. Night came over dark but fine, and when we made out the glimmer of the outer lightship ahead, I sent both Hescroff and the long-suffering Dutchman below, taking the first watch myself. The Mate sat up with me smoking. Nothing occurred to break the quiet monotony of the night, except a lurid glare enlivened by occasional ascents of a rocket on the horizon, where Heligoland had appeared at sunset. One or two big steamers also rushed by at a distance, their red, green, and white lamps gleaming like meteors as they went. The breeze remained so gentle and steady, that we carried the topsail all night through, and, making capital progress, rounded the light-vessel against a strong ebb tide, at five minutes to one on Saturday morning. The Mate had turned in two hours earlier, and I now called up Hescroff to take his watch, retiring into the cabin myself.

When I came on deck again at six o'clock the Widgeon had reached a point about two miles above the port of Cuxhaven. A very light breeze aft was gently propelling her towards Brunsbüttel, with the aid of the current on the flood. Hescroff told me that the weather had continued quiet and fine ever since I had gone below, and that as we passed the inner light-vessel, he had noticed her swinging to the change of tide.

I looked around, pleased and surprised. Close on our starboard hand was a green wooded shore, studded here and there with church spires and red house-roofs, above the verdant dykes which protect the low lands of Hanover from the rising Elbe. Further inland could be dimly espied the first hills we had seen since passing Cape Gris Nez. Ships there were in plenty scattered on the broad surface of the river, some at anchor, some sailing our way, and many flying the old British red ensign. The fresh air of the morning, just warmed with the rays of the rising sun, and the swift-escaping mist, promised a hot and clear-eyed day.

The channel is deep, wide, and easily navigated, but the failing wind retarded our progress. At eight o'clock, however, after breakfast, we found ourselves not more than three miles from Brunsbüttel, but to leeward, and the wind having veered, had to make a tack to reach it.

But little is to be seen of Brunsbüttel from the Elbe, except the white painted lighthouse perched on the inevitable interminable dyke, and the church spire, plated with copper of a bright verdigris hue, in startling semi-contrast with the deep green heads of the surrounding trees. The harbour entrance, which is marked by a small beacon, is no wider than a narrow canal, and being swept at right angles by the tide, it is necessary to keep very close to the port bank in entering on the flood. We were on the point of anchoring to reconnoitre, when a fisherman, who introduced himself to me as " Claus Wolff," in a few words of broken English, boarded us, and fixing a rope on the bowsprit end, towed the Widgeon in. The wind had fallen quite away, so we punted her along easily for a quarter of a mile, as far as a quay where the harbour widens enough to allow a small steamer to turn round.

Our approach had been telegraphed from Cuxhaven, and a crowd of the inhabitants, who had been expecting us for weeks, watched our entry and

scrutinised us with great curiosity.   In a few minutes
my brother also came up, with Dr. Wolff, the Haupt
pastor, whose acquaintance I then had the pleasure
of making for the first time.

After a dispute with the pilot, who claimed more
than his due, but was paid off at last with his
expenses back to Ostmahorn, and a few thalers over
and above his government allowance, we all proceeded into the village together.

Brunsbüttel is built in two parts, which are quite
separate and fully half a mile distant from one
another.   Constructed on the dyke, at the head of
the little port, stand the principal inn and most of the
new houses, about none of which is there anything
remarkable.   Passing these we found ourselves in a
straight high-road, bordered with young cherry trees,
and parted from the black soil of the rich corn fields
on either side by ditches full of water.   At the end
of this road lies old Brunsbüttel, consisting of a
square of moderate-sized, substantially built red
brick tenements, with low-pitched roofs that spring
from just above the ground floor windows.   In the
midst, on a small green, over-shadowed by massy
elms, the little church uprears its humble spire, plated
with copper from the wreck of a ship.

One other monument shares with the house of
God the distinction of a place on the village green,

and that is a small stone obelisk, which bears the names of five Brunsbüttelers, who fell in the French war.   The simple inscription runs thus :—

"Den Heldentod für's Vaterland starben im grossem Kriege 1870-1871."

Then follow the names.   On the other side are the words :—

"Zur Ehre den Todten ; Zur Vorbild der Jugend : Zur Erinnerung Allen."

A few steps from the obelisk brought us to the door of the parsonage, where we had received a kind invitation from Dr. Wolff to stay as long as our visit to Brunsbüttel lasted.

CHAPTER XXII.

BRUNSBÜTTEL.

Sunday morning service—" Dr. Martinus Luther "—Piratical exploits of the ancient Brunsbüttelers—The Reformation in Dithmarschen—Boje family—Dr. Johannes Angelus Arcimbold—Martyrdom of Heinrich of Zütphen—Old war song—Inundations—Legend of the church-bells—Flood of 1719—Rebuilding of the dyke—Sail to Cuxhaven.

THE service in the church at Brunsbüttel on Sunday morning, is of a simple yet solemn character. Amid surroundings which descend from an earlier tradition, the plain black robe and white starched ruff in which the clergyman officiates, bear the stamp of higher associations than those which hover about modern ecclesiastical millinery. Out of his dark frame hanging on the whitewashed wall, "Doctor Martinus Luther," limned by some old native artist, looks down approvingly on his undegenerate followers with fixed and moveless eyes. A few homely prayers and ancient hymns are offered up, a quiet, effective sermon is delivered, and then the villagers troop forth to enjoy a true day of rest. The door closes when the neighbouring landed proprietors, last of the congregation, have rolled away in their family coaches. Worship is then over for the week. Sunday afternoon is the time for making visits, for amusement and relaxation. Early on Monday morning every man will be out again in the fields ploughing, sowing, or reaping, according to the season.

So passes life at Brunsbüttel from week to week, from twelvemonth to twelvemonth, from century to century. Still, it must not be imagined that the quaint little place has no history of its own.

It was not until many months after the cruise was over that I came across an interesting pamphlet, of which the learned Hauptpastor is the author. It is the substance of two lectures delivered by him for the benefit of the inhabitants of Schleswig-Holstein, who were ruined by the flood of the 10th and 17th of December, 1872. I need make no apology for introducing into this chapter some account of places, persons, and events, many of which, but for Dr. Wolff's labours, would doubtless have sunk into oblivion.

The earliest known documents relating to the history of Brunsbüttel are of·a singular description, being nothing less than treaties of peace between this insignificant little town and the great commercial city of Hamburg! Gravesend.making war upon London would be a parallel case. ·

In 1286, five families in Brunsbüttel leagued them-

selves with five others in Marne, a village some miles
to the north-west, and began war against Hamburg
merchantmen passing up and down the Elbe. It was
war that bordered very closely upon piracy, and the
bellicose Brunsbüttelers got off cheaply, after a sea-
fight in which they were worsted, by merely being
compelled to swear never to molest any merchant for
the future. In spite of this they broke out again in
1308, when, excited by ancient blood-feuds, four
families rejoicing in the quaint names of Amezinghe,
Boken, Etzinghe and Zerzinghe Mannen, once more
leagued themselves against Hamburg. For seven
years their predatory outrages were endured, but at
last the merchants of the Hanse town attacked them
in force, and getting the best of a battle, in which
there were many killed and wounded on both sides,
carried off a few prisoners, whom they proceeded at
once to shorten by the head.

After a sack and burning of Brunsbüttel by one
Claus Engel, in 1491, the next historical event of any
importance occurred in connection with the spread of
the Reformation in Dithmarschen, by which name the
whole eastern side of Holstein is known. The history
of this phenomenon is also closely interwoven with
that of a family yclept " Boje."

In 1500, Marcus Boje was living at Nordhusen, a
hamlet in the vicinity. He was a man of considerable

wealth and dignity, tracing his descent from one
Baje Boje, who, about the year 1208, held the ferry at
Brunsbüttel in fief of the Archbishop of Bremen, and
levied from Oester-moor, another hamlet, a tribute
of one hen from each household. This was known as
the "Rauch-huhn," or "smoke-hen," each chimney
being reckoned as representing a house.

Marcus Boje had seven sons, on whom he bestowed
a good education, with the express object of enabling
them to aid in the rectification of certain errors in the
Roman Catholic Church.

About the year 1517, when the ninety-five theses,
which Luther had nailed on the door of Wittenberg
Cathedral, became known at Brunsbüttel, Boje despatched his sons Nicolaus and Boethius, to profit by
the teaching of the great Reformer, with whom
Nicolaus presently cemented a lasting friendship. In
1524 he was made pastor of Meldorf, a small town
not far away.

The most important of all the circumstances that
were, about this time, conspiring to prepare the
ground in Dithmarschen, for the new doctrines of the
Reformation, was the shameless trade of the indul-
gence-vendor, Doctor Johannes Angelus Arcimbold.
This personage held a licence to sell all kinds of
papal dispensations in France, Germany and Sweden.
The profits of his traffic, in which he employed as

sub-agents five Dithmarschen priests, were so enormous, that he could afford to travel with gold and silver pots and pans, while even his chests had golden locks. The latter, however, were painted over in oil-colours, "that they might not glitter too much in the eyes of the desperate covetous."

Doctor Arcimbold's proceedings had scandalized everybody in Meldorf, who had previously entertained any objection to papistry. Nicolaus Boje, the pastor, spoke so forcibly in condemnation as to induce Augustin Torneborg, abbot of grey friars, to write to Bremen that he outdid Luther himself, and so wrought upon the people, that they were actually beginning to dispute with his monks on points of doctrine. A widow of good family, named Wiebe Junge, zealously took up the new teaching. She prevailed upon Boje to invite to Meldorf Heinrich of Zütphen, a noted Lutheran, the story of whose labour and martyrdom is one of deep and painful interest.

In spite of dissuasion on the part of his friends, Heinrich disembarked at Brunsbüttel in November, 1524, from Bremen, and reached Meldorf shortly after. There abbot Torneborg at once raised a strong opposition. He even succeeded in persuading the Council of Forty-eight, who then administered the affairs of Dithmarschen, to decree the banishment both of Heinrich and Nicolaus Boje. The former, notified of this decree, cried out : " Should I die here, heaven is as nigh in Dithmarsch as elsewhere, and I doubt not but that, some time or another, I must seal the Gospel with a bloody death ! " Finding that their commands were not obeyed, the Forty-eight, after a stormy discussion, decided to let things remain as they were, until after the General Council. The concluding words of their resolution display a most rare and uncommon trust in other people : " what our neighbours adopt and believe, that will we also."

Disappointed at the turn affairs have taken, the monks raised a mob to attack Heinrich, which gathered at Henningstedt, on the tenth of December, 1524, under cover of the night.

" Five hundred peasants had been summoned together (I am now quoting the Hauptpastor's pamphlet), for whose behoof three tuns of Hamburg beer were broached. To their criminal deed they armed themselves with fiendish ingenuity ; drunkenness, that friend of the wicked, and foe of all good emotions, was pressed into the service of the conspirators ; and the shadows of night, which had already concealed the birth and growth of the plot, convoyed the armed mob to the dwelling of Nicolaus Boje.

" In order to obtain admission into the house, they

had looked about them for a traitor, and found him
in the person of a man called Henning Hans. This
fellow daily frequented the parsonage, and now
opened a trapdoor in the ground to the enemies of
his master. A man of Wakenhusen strode into the
house, and opened the door from the inside, whereupon the wild crowd surged in, swearing and brawl-
ing, with incessant cries of 'Hau dodt! Hau dodt!'

"Nicolaus Boje was torn out of bed, beaten, and
dragged naked into the street, where he was left un-
noticed to lie. Heinrich was bound, and constrained
in the winter-cold to walk on the hard-frozen roads
over snow and ice towards Heide. Soon his feet
were mangled by the ice; he begged earnestly for a
horse, but in vain: they scoffed at and abused him
outrageously. To save appearances, he was brought
before a tribunal, and condemned to death by fire.

"On the eleventh of December, 1524, at eight
o'clock in the morning, Heinrich was taken into the
market-place of Heide. His sentence, which was
there read out, recited, 'This Villain has preached
against the Mother of God, and the Christian Faith,
for which reasons, on the authority of his Reverence
the Bishop of Bremen, he is condemned to the flames.'

"The only answer to these words that Heinrich
made was, 'That have I not done;' and to the sum-
mons to submission, 'Thy will be accomplished!'

"Wiebe Junge begged earnestly for a delay of at least three days in the execution of the sentence; even offering a thousand guilders for the grant of such a respite, but her supplications were not acceded to, and the mob stamped upon the suppliant with their feet. For two hours long the flame of the pyre would not blaze, whereupon they bound Heinrich to a ladder, so that the blood gushed forth from his mouth and nose. A man tried to set the ladder on end, and prop it up with his halberd, but it slipped, and the halberd went through the back of the tortured victim. At last, a blow from a hammer, directed against him by a man named Johann Holm, put a period to his sufferings.

"Thus died this highly-gifted preacher of the gospel, at the age of thirty-six years. His head, his hands, and feet were cut off, and burnt on live charcoal, the trunk was buried, and then savage dancing around the pyre concluded the awful revel. Luther himself has written the story of Heinrich of Zütphen, and addressed special epistles of condolence to his parishioners at Bremen and Meldorf, as well as to Wiebe Junge."

This martyrdom, like most others, completely failed of the anticipated effect, for the seed of the Reformation began at once to take firmer root than ever. The family of the Bojes kept it alive, and watched it growing into a strong luxuriant plant. Nicolaus survived the death of his friend Heinrich more than twenty years. He was the first clergyman in Dithmarsch who ever married. Boethius Boje became Hauptpastor of Brunsbüttel in 1561, and died in 1565, at the ripe age of seventy,

In the year 1531 a panic arose in Dithmarschen, upon a rumour that Friedrich I. of Denmark was going to invade the country. A watch was posted at Brunsbüttel, but the alarm proved false, and nothing came of it but a revulsion of feeling, which produced this curious old Platt Deutsch song :—

" Dar is ein nie Raht geraden,
  Tho Rostorpe up der Heide
Dat hebben de Acht und Vertig gedaen,
  De besten in unsen Lande,
Dat dar scholden viffundert Man
  Tho Brunsbüttel up der Wachte.
Claes Marcus Hergen stund im Dore,
  He sprak : Gott si gelavet !
Ik seh so mannigen finen Man
  Von Norden her gedravet.
Se togen ein lüttik bi Dikelang,
  Wol na der Dikes Horne ;
Dar schlogen se de Speisen schwank,
  Wol na der Landsknecht Wise
Wiben Peter und Claes Marx Hergen
  De schoten de groten Büssen aff,
Dartho de witten Schlangen
  Se stelden de Büssen upt Sandt
Se schoten over in dat Kedinger Land
  Den Kedingern den wardt bange.

> Dat hebben de Dithmarscher Buren gedahn
>   Se mögen wol Heren wesen.
> Leven se noch söven Jare
>   Dithmarschen worden Landesheren."

The song may be literally interpreted thus :—

> There is a new counsel counselled
>   At Rostorp, up the Heath,*
> That have the Eight and Forty done,
>   The best in our land :
> That there should five hundred men
>   To Brunsbüttel on the watch.
> Claes Marcus Hergen stood at his door,
>   He said : "Now God be lauded !
> I see so many fine men
>   From Norden hither ordered."
> They bode a little at Dikelang,
>   Quite near the dykes' horn.
> There beat they the victuals soft,†
>   Just like the lancer's way.
> Wiben Peter and Claus Marx Hergen
>   They shot the great busses off,
> Also the white serpents
>   The busses they set up on the sand,‡
> They shot over into the Kedinger land,
>   To the Kedingers then came fright.
> That have the Dithmarsch boors done,
>   They might well be gentlemen.
> Live they yet seven years
>   Dithmarschen's masters they may be.

---

* The interior of Holstein is heath-land, very sandy and barren ; the fertile soil of Dithmarschen is only a fringe of mud recovered from the Elbe.

† In the barges on the Elbe, men may be seen pounding away with sticks at the dry salt-fish to make it soft enough to eat.

‡ The "busses" were evidently cannon. The word occurs in "blunderbuss."

Evidently the Dithmarsch "boors" had a good opinion of themselves. It is amusing to read of their spite against "dat Kedinger Land" on the opposite coast of Hanover, with which they were continually at loggerheads.

Nearly thirty years later, Dithmarschen lost its independence, falling under the sway of Friedrich II. of Denmark, in 1559. A visitation of the plague afflicted Brunsbüttel in 1605, when Marcus Boje died, who was then Hauptpastor. From this date, until 1630, the ravages of the plague appear to have been almost incessant; but they were eclipsed by the calamities which overwhelmed the land in the shape of terrible inundations, and occupation by cruel enemies. Wallenstein, the Swedes, the Danes, and the Hamburgers, in succession pillaged and burnt at will, until peace was declared in 1645. Even the insignificant respite which followed was interrupted by a fearful famine in 1651, and panics continued to agitate the minds of the broken-spirited population until 1660, when the peace of Copenhagen was concluded. Famine, plague, and war had now done their worst: the total ruin of the ancient village was to be consummated by the great river to which it owed its very being.

Disastrous floods are recorded as having taken place in the years 1566, 1617, 1628, 1656, and 1664, upon each of which occasions many houses were destroyed and large tracts of land rendered barren by salt water, or buried under the waves. However the most memorable of all these catastrophes occurred in 1674, when, by an extraordinary tide, Brunsbüttel* was completely blotted out of existence!

The church itself is the chief memorial of this great flood, although partly ruined by lightning, and rebuilt some fifty years later. It stands far away from the ancient site of the sacred edifice, and, like the ark of Noah, has perched itself upon the highest elevation within reach. Embedded in its outer wall may be discovered a stone tablet, four or five feet square, sculptured in bas-relief with a rude figure of St. James, and bearing an inscription to the effect that the church was begun to be rebuilt in 1677, and that the first sermon was preached within its walls in November of the same year.

The saintly patron of the church is portrayed with a most ferocious countenance, wearing a thick moustache from ear to ear. The cast of his features reminded me of some rude gargoyles in old Norman churches, in which the artist was not consciously labouring after grotesqueness.

---

* Anciently called Braunsbüttel. *But* = *Theil,* a part or share : *tel* is the diminutive. The place therefore is in all probability named after some former possessor, *Braun* or Bruno.—*Dr. Wolff.*

Part of the bare outer walls enveloping this quaint memorial, a pulpit, and the font, were all that was rescued from destruction, when, in 1719, the church was laid in ashes by a stroke of lightning, which fell while the pastor was in the act of delivering his homily. This disaster took years to repair, and the present building was only completed in 1724.

It contains a fine carved pulpit, not the original one saved out of the fire, but one executed by the artist-carpenters, Hans Eckermann and Hans Reyer, of Hamburg. The same workmen executed a fine bold relief in wood of the arms of Denmark, to adorn the royal pew, which the parishioners erected in gratitude for the help afforded them by King Friedrich, in subscribing money towards the rebuilding of the church.

The altar-piece, a lofty wooden structure, set with twelve oval medallions carved in high relief, representing scriptural events, was bought out of Glückstadt Cathedral. This work of art is unfortunately disfigured by a dense coating of churchwarden's whitewash.

An interesting legend accounts for the absence of a set of chimes. Those naughty Kedingers, it appears, availed themselves of the moment of general misery caused by the great flood, to steal the Brunsbüttel church-bells, which were large and rich in tone. An

exasperated Brunsbütteler, powerless to prevent the
theft, cried after them this curse :—

> " Fortan soll euer Klang es sagen,
>   Wem ihr gehört in frühern Tagen ;
>   Bis die Kedinger ihr Land unter Wasser sehn
>   Und ins Kedinger Land die Dithmarscher gehn,
>   Sollt ihr jammern und zagen,
>   Sollt ihr stöhnen und klagen,
>   ' Nach Brunsbüttel ! '
>   ' Nach Brunsbüttel ! ' "

This may be rhythmically rendered in English :—

> Henceforth shall your clamour say,
>   Whose you were at a former day :
>   Till the Kedingers their land under water view,
>   And to Kedinger land the Dithmarschers go too,
>   Shall you grumble and chatter,
>   Shall you murmur and clatter,
>   "To Brunsbüttel ! "
>   "To Brunsbüttel! "

When the Kedingers got home, they hung up
their booty in the church tower at Balje, and the
bells promptly began to carry out the terms of the
curse. Every time they were tolled, they thundered
out " Nach Brunsbüttel ! Nach Brunsbüttel ! " and it
was even believed that when foul weather was at hand
they sounded louder than usual, to give warning to
their old friends on the other side of the river. Only
in 1825 was the curse loosed. In this year a winter
flood severed the village of Balje from the mainland. The water became covered with a thin coat of

ice, not strong enough to bear up men, but forming an
effectual bar to access by boats. Now was the time
for the Brunsbüttelers to come for vengeance. They
crossed the Elbe, landed without accident, and supplied the starving people with clothes and provisions.
When they departed, the bells were left at Balje still,
but their chimes are now no longer fraught with re-
minders of the ancient grudge.

After the inundation of 1674, Brunsbüttel was rebuilt as it now stands, nearly a mile away from the
original site, which was probably close to the harbour.
Fresh onslaughts of the waves assailed the new locality
in 1684 and 1699, and there still exists a piteous catalogue of houses and acres reft away by the sea.

Worse misfortune yet overtook the parish on
Christmas eve, 1717, when "a fierce gale with heavy
rain" arose, "which in the night flew round to the
north-west, and impelled a mass of water with such
force against the dyke, that this bulwark burst. Instead of merry peals, the dismal toll of the storm-bells
moaned over the land, that lay all covered up in
water. Through this flood was the loss of a hundred
and seventy-three lives to be deplored; sixty-two
buildings fell in, two hundred houses were damaged,
and a vast extent of land was rendered unfruitful by
the salt water. The most bitter want reigned among
the parishioners. All taxes were necessarily remitted.

Every inhabitant, both of the marshes and higher
lands, was enjoined to labour on the dyke. Dragoons
were quartered in the neighbouring parishes, in order
to compel to work all such persons as refused their
aid. The king sent a present of large trees, with
which to dam up the Eddelack breach. Twice was
the dyke entirely restored; twice was it again completely obliterated in parts, by the untameable billows
of the sea. As a consequence of this, on the thirty-
first of December, 1719, the place was again flooded
over. This time King Friedrich IV. despatched
Colonel Jobst von Scholten with five hundred soldiers,
to join the dwellers in the Wilstermarsch in raising
up the dyke once more. The old line of the battered
rampart was given up in despair, leaving over to be
the sport of the wild waves, seven hundred and
seventy-two morgen of land.*" The new dyke which
was then constructed derives from its builders the
name of "Soldatendeich," but lies considerably to
landward of the more modern coast defences.

Passing to the harbour along the summit of the
dyke on Sunday, and looking down on the calm
Elbe-stream lapping its base quite thirty feet below,
I could scarcely credit that such a barrier could ever
be overborne. However, it must be remembered that
in mediæval times and even later, it was neither so

---

* More than two thousand acres.

P

elevated, so strong, nor so scientifically constructed, as now. Moreover, repairs were seldom given beforehand to avert catastrophes, but only after they had occurred.

The dyke, like the disused fortifications of many continental towns, forms a capital promenade. It is dry and comfortable to walk upon, unlike the fields below, through which it is the custom to lay narrow paths of bricks, two abreast. Without this precaution, in rainy seasons it would become almost impossible to stray off the main roads.

It was about three o'clock in the afternoon, when we reached the Widgeon, and in the finest of weather leisurely sailed with a fair complement of ladies on board, down the river nearly to Cuxhaven. Then, on turning back, we passed close under the stern of a coal-laden schooner. Hailing her, "What ship's that?" the captain answered, "Elizabeth of Pwhelli; three weeks out." His Welsh crew appeared very surprised at meeting us in the Elbe.

The Widgeon soon left the collier astern, and rapidly caught all the other craft bound the same way, but did not land us at Brunsbüttel until after dark in the evening; wind and tide both proving unfavourable.

CHAPTER XXIII.

BRUNSBÜTTEL.

The sturgeon fishery—The coppersmith's wedding—Agricultural society —A grand funeral—Subjects of conversation—Sport in Dith- marschen.—The game of "Boszel"—"Almightys"—The dyke— Land reclaimed from the Elbe—Storks' nests.

HAVING dilated, perhaps at too great length, on the bygone struggles of Brunsbüttel, my story would be incomplete without some reference to the details of its present life. For example, it may be mentioned without any betrayal of confidence, that some of the delicacies enjoyed by the good Brunsbüttelers are eels cured in smoke, and uncooked ham subjected to the same process. What other dainties are peculiar to different seasons of the year, I cannot tell; but caviare, at least, can be no rarity where sturgeon are caught in so great abundance. These truculent seeming, but really dull and pacific monsters of the sea, are snared by the local fishermen with nets, in little, round-bowed, high-sided boats, built for that especial purpose. As for common food, there is no lack of beef, the product of the rich alluvial pastures; but Hamburg is ready to buy all the cattle that can be bred, and so the Brunsbüttelers have to pay a long price. The beef, if not the mutton, of Dithmarsch is good enough to stand on its own merits, and so it should be, considering the trouble and expense the farmers have been at, in importing cattle from England wherewith to cross their own stock. In this matter and in the introduction of English farming implements, Herr Maassen, the largest landowner in the parish, has taken a leading part. The smallness of the holdings, which rarely much exceed a hundred acres in extent, has rendered a system of mutual co-operation necessary to the farmers, who singly would be unable to bear the expense of many valuable aids to the saving of labour. They have, therefore, constituted an agricultural society, which purchases whatever machinery or breeding stock the committee may determine to acquire, and lets it out in rotation to the individual members.

Brunsbüttel has now been free from serious inundations for nearly a hundred years. Salt impregnations have disappeared from the soil, which, once relieved from their growth-stunting influence, displays unchecked its natural fertility. Rich, deep, and damp, and cultivated with untiring energy, the fields return a golden wage, and really it seems astonishing what considerable fortunes are reputed to have been amassed in agriculture. Signs of comparative afflu-

ence, indeed, are not wanting in Brunsbüttel. From
time to time new houses are built, always with more
ambitious architectural embellishments than of yore.
Two smart little new iron screw-steamers may be
seen lying in the haven, in the intervals when they
are not employed in carrying cattle, goods, and
passengers backwards and forwards between Brunsbüttel and Hamburg. Colliers from Newcastle or
Middlesborough not unfrequently put in with cargoes
consigned to some retired sea-captain, or rich farmer,
who does not live wholly idle, or altogether engrossed
in his primary occupation. One or two fine clipper
brigs even, make their number off Brunsbüttel, in
dropping down the Elbe on a voyage perhaps to
the China seas. Their proud owners, with very
different feelings from those which actuated their
fellow-townsmen of the thirteenth century,* watch
them from the shore, and wish them good luck out
and a good freight home. Wealth does not glitter in
Dithmarschen, but is displayed in sober, substantial
possessions. It was my good fortune to witness the
funeral of an old personage of consideration in the
land. His body was convoyed to its last resting-
place by no less than eight and twenty coaches,
each drawn by two sturdy, broad-hoofed cart-horses,
and containing all that was most weighty and most

* Vide *supra.*

respectable in the country side. Some of the vehicles were certainly such as could not now-a-days be found in a hurry elsewhere. Vast erections, ponderous heirlooms; I dare not fix their age! Others were of elegant modern construction, but appeared less in keeping with the air and spirit of the place than their aged but still serviceable brethren. However, it is evident that Brunsbüttel prospers in these latter days, and will not lag behind the world.

Certainly it is, and will always remain, a little dull: but then, is not even dulness better than lightning and tempest, than plague, pestilence, and famine, than battle and murder, and than sudden death? At any rate, the Brunsbüttelers of to-day do not grudge their ancestors these amenities.

Nevertheless, they too have their excitements. For instance, not long before the novelty of our arrival, there had occurred three suicides in rapid succession. The first was that of a foolish young man, who considerately came by steamer from Hamburg, where his proceedings would not have attracted much attention, and blew his brains out with a pistol in the bedroom of an inn. The other two, I believe, were perpetrated by disinterested Brunsbüttelers, for the sole purpose of alleviating the monotony of their fellow-townsmen's lives.

Again, after winter gales, the corpses of sailors are

not unfrequently washed ashore. Not very long ago, a sturgeon-fisherman picked up one at sea, and carried it into the haven. Now the parish has to pay the cost of interment for all bodies cast up in the ordinary course of events, but this particular one had come in a most irregular manner. Might it not have landed of its own accord at Cuxhaven, at Glückstadt, or anywhere else, had not the fool of a fisherman opened his eyes too wide? Certainly it might. Again, might it not have been only one of a hundred brought ashore at Brunsbüttel, from some great emigrant ship wrecked in sight of home? Why, that contingency was too frightful to think of—it would ruin the parish! Here was opportunity for a petition to the Government, praying for reimbursement of the burial charges, that no precedent for such a ruinous practice might inadvertently arise. The petition was presented, but what the Government said in reply is not upon my notes.

There is an amusing story of a wedding, which exhibits the character of the people in a pleasant light. A certain coppersmith, whose head contained more ambitious than reasonable ideas, conceived a wish to marry. He was not blessed with many worldly goods, which perhaps made him the more anxious to take unto himself a wife who was. His mode of procedure was, to say the least, eccentric.

It consisted in applying, one by one, to the best families in the neighbourhood for the hand of an heiress, and so to run down the scale till the offer was accepted. By this means he fancied he would secure, if not the most eligible young lady in the parish, at any rate the best he could have. Accordingly, after a visit of inquiry to the pastor, who was not, however, entrusted with the whole secret, he trudged in his most resplendent suit of clothes to all the richest landowners in succession.

Everyone was prepared; the plan had oozed out long before it was put into execution; all were in raptures at the honour he proposed to confer upon them, but each felt himself unworthy to become the father-in-law of so distinguished an individual. The poor man was flattered, but, at his wits' end for a wife, continued his matrimonial tour until he reached the house of a rich old farmer, who had a particularly handsome daughter. The conventional question was put, and he could scarcely believe his ears when the reply came, "Only ask the girl; for my part, there is nothing I should like better than to confer my daughter upon you." The infatuated fellow, never doubting for one moment of success, dashed out into the garden, where this lovely young lady was engaged in picking peas, and without further ado, asked her to marry him. Alas for his vanity, never did unfortunate lover receive so point-blank a rebuff. Our hero retired completely discomfited, and in the first blush of chagrin paid his addresses to a woman in his own rank of life. They were crowned with success, and the time for the wedding approached before the aspiring coppersmith had taken thought for the morrow. A brain so fertile in expedients, however, soon hit upon a scheme for raising the wind. To show that he bore no malice, all the personages for whose daughters' hands he had applied were invited to his wedding. They came, and after the ceremony was over, were regaled with abundance of good cheer. Then, and not till then, while his guests were full of laughter and jollity, the wily coppersmith sent round his hat! To the credit of the company, although taken by surprise, they returned it to the lucky couple with a good round sum in silver in the crown, which not only paid the expenses of the feast, but left a good many thalers over, as a marriage portion for the wife.

Of sport there is but little in Dithmarschen, for reasons not difficult to imagine. Game is scarce, and the fishing is hardly worth having, but in the winter plenty of wild fowl, and occasionally stray seals, are to be met with. In the same season, when the ground is like pavement, and the ditches are frozen hard, so that the country can be crossed at will, the game of "Boszel" is played.

The chief peculiarity of this local diversion is the ball, which is the only implement used, and a curious one it is too. A carpenter turns a sphere of wood, bores holes like those in the outer skin of the Chinese ivory globes within globes, and fills them up with melted lead. The result is a "boszel." So far so easy: but to use the boszel to advantage must, I imagine (for I never saw the game played), require a considerable amount of practice and training.

My brother describes the game thus: Two sides are picked out of opposing villages, each group of peasants gathers at the starting point, one man heaves the boszel with all his might in front of him, all rush after it in a body, and where it stops another of his party picks it up and sets the ball rolling again. The other side follow suit, and over ditch, dyke, and meadow they blunder, panting on, till the goal is reached, perhaps eight or nine miles away. Whichever village has accomplished the distance in the fewest throws, wins; and then comes an immediate adjournment to some inn, where, amid pipes and beer, the battle is fought over again, till from words they sometimes come to blows, and at night both victors and vanquished wend sorrowfully home. Evidently it is a capital game, boszel, and one that stimulates courage, muscle, and wind.

One reason for the rarity of sports and pastimes in Dithmarschen, is the absence of any aristocracy, or any class of men whose time hangs idle on their hands. The largest landed proprietor in Brunsbüttel holds about three hundred acres, and the average acreage of what are esteemed considerable estates, is about one hundred and fifty. Such properties receive the owner's personal supervision and even manual toil, for day labourers are both scarce and expensive. Before its conquest by the Danes, Dithmarschen was a republic, the affairs of which were administered by an elective council of forty-eight members, whose necessary qualification was the possession of at least ten morgen (30 acres) of land. This institution still survives, but for some time has exercised only a local authority, resembling that of boards of guardians in England. The members are addressed as "Voll-macht." It would appear more reasonable (*pace* Sir Charles Dilke*) to search for "Barons" at Corfe Castle than "Almightys" at Brunsbüttel; neverthe-less, while the former are wholly extinct, the latter are very far from being so. Even now, the title of "Vollmacht" is an honourable distinction, and to be

* Vide his speech in the House on " Unreformed Corporations," reported in the *Times* of March 1st, 1876.

the wife of one, is to be envied amongst women! It is remarkable how little visible impress two centuries of Danish rule have left among those people, at least, who live on the outskirts of Süder Dithmarschen. Still there were dissentients when, as part of Schleswig-Holstein, it was appropriated in 1864 by Prussia; although it might have been imagined that people who had spoken "Platt Deutsch" from time immemorial, would not manifest any repugnance towards forsaking the wing of Denmark. It was probably heavy taxes that they feared; and then there loomed behind the shadow of universal conscription. They were frightened at the shadow; what do they think of the reality?—a burden upon all Germany almost too great to bear, but which absolutely must be endured.

One more characteristic, which might have been expected to be strongly developed among the Brunsbüttelers—ever-present anxiety—is nevertheless absent. I should have thought it difficult for them to dwell without a certain solicitude below the level of a vast river, which time after time broke through their forefathers' defences, to slay in one tide more than in ten long years fell victims to age, disease, or war. Yet they do live in careless confidence, founded partly on long impunity, and partly on the strength of the dyke, which is now kept in permanent order by a staff of workmen, under the command of resident engineers. In the course of a visit of some days' duration, I had the pleasure of being accompanied along the dyke by one of these gentlemen, Herr Krönke, who is in charge of many miles of the great sea-wall from Brunsbüttel down the Elbe to seaward. He explained that one great object in its construction is to obtain a fair outline, without re-entrant angles, or projections of any description, which are sure to be first attacked by the sea. The upper part is all kept sedulously covered with close green turf, which prevents the soil from being washed loose. Where once this turf is removed the waves very quickly eat their way in. Any loss of earth is replaced in the breach directly the tide allows, and covered thickly over with ropes of straw pegged tightly down. Under this protection, by the time the straw rots away, a fresh coating of grass has grown up.

The base of the dyke, which enters the water at a much more obtuse angle than that presented by the superstructure, is covered with large boulders. Nothing illustrates more pertinently than the history of these stones, the immense amount of labour, time, and money expended annually on the mere means of preserving the land from the sea. Every stone has been grappled for from the bottom of the Baltic, by vessels which go there through the Eider canal, a

average voyage of six weeks out and back. Surely
Portland or Purbeck could supply stone at a cheaper
rate than this must entail. There is a curious tradition, by the way, at Swanage, which gives ground for
a belief that not very long ago, stone actually did find
its way over from thence. An old seaman, who is
now dead, told me that when he was young, the
" Dutch " used to come over and ship boulders off
the beach, at a place called Punfield Cove, on the
north side of Swanage Bay. He said also that there
was formerly a pond at the foot of the cliff; but that
after the removal of a great number of stones which
lay between it and the sea, either the latter en-
croached, or the pond burst out, so that no trace of
it now remains but a piece of level marshy ground.
The appearance of the spot, as well as the name
Punfield,* fully bears out the story, and the seafaring
people of Dithmarschen are quite likely to have been
confounded with the Dutch.

The efforts of the engineers of Holstein are not
merely directed towards protecting the land which
already exists, but to rescuing new tracts from the
alluvial foreshores. One of these acquisitions of
territory lies only a few miles from Brunsbüttel, and
although the land is hardly dry, the greater part has
been already taken up, and parcelled into rectangular

* = Pond field.

farms.   At regular intervals the treeless waste is dotted with bran-new brick buildings, interspersed among scanty, verdant crops, fighting for very existence with the caked salt exudations of the slimy half-drained soil.

Overlooking this wilderness barely parted from the sea, it excited wonder to behold the hardy men who had come to live there, firmly trusting to spend their lives upon it in security and peace.   Many had already fixed upon the gables of their high-pitched roofs, the carved crosspieces of wood which it is the custom in Friesland and Dithmarschen to erect for the storks, to encourage a gentle pair of those luck-breeding birds to build their nest between!

CHAPTER XXIV.

BRUNSBÜTTEL BY THE ELBE TO HAMBURG.

En route — Glückstadt — Ice-rams — Schwarz-tonnen sand — The "Goethe" and "Schiller"—"John" and "Nicholas Smirk"— "Fischer-ewers"—Wedel, Schulau, Blankenese—Altona—First glimpse of Hamburg.

FROM the dyke at Brunsbüttel it is but one step to the harbour, and there on Monday morning, the 27th of July, lay the Widgeon with sails loose, awaiting our party, which this time was increased by the presence of my brother and Dr. Wolff. A careful man, named Thode, had been engaged as pilot for the sail to Hamburg, with whose help our little ship soon was punted out of the harbour. At twenty minutes past eight she was off under all plain sail, with a fresh breeze over the quarter, and crossed the bows of the screw-collier "George Eliot," which with the British pilot-jack fluttering aloft, was wandering slowly up the river. In an hour's time we had made a progress of nearly nine miles, and were abeam of the Glückstadt Sand, a low mud islet, flooded by unusually high tides, but generally eight or even ten feet out of water, and overgrown with willows, reeds, and the rankest of grass. Not long afterwards we passed Glückstadt, a town of little importance and dwindling into less, now that it no longer remains the Danish rival of Hamburg. It possesses a fine harbour, yet ships are said hardly ever to put in there, except occasionally, when stopped by the ice which blocks the Elbe every winter.

This annual impediment to the navigation of the river, must be a serious drawback to the commerce of Hamburg. Until recently no effectual means of alleviating its effects were available ; but now, by means of a steam ram, fitted with iron-plated bows for charging the accumulations of ice, the river is rendered passable both later and earlier than heretofore. Indeed the success of a small craft employed in this manner, by a few of the leading merchants and shipowners, has proved so encouraging as to prompt the construction of a larger and more powerful vessel for future service. Nothing shows more clearly the advantages of England's oceanic climate, than the fact that the great river Elbe, in about the same latitude as Hull, is completely encumbered with ice during some of the winter months.

Off Glückstadt it became necessary to tack, and cross over to the other side. The land here lies very low, and is only protected from the tides by lofty turf-clad embankments, the foreshores of which often extend so far, as to give them the appearance of being situated miles inland.   At five minutes to eleven, Schwarz-tonnen Sand was reached—a long low isle, adorned with a huge black beacon, from which its name is derived.   Round the extremity of this obstruction, the main channel narrows to little more than a hundred yards in width, and takes a remarkably sharp turn southwards for a quarter of a mile, after which its former direction is resumed.   Vessels can almost run their bowsprits over the shore without grounding, so steep are the banks, washed by a tide running so fast, that even with a stiff breeze, the Widgeon had some difficulty in stemming it.   Large steamers find the corner very hard to turn.   They are obliged to rush at it full speed, and alter their helms very smartly, to avoid running on the shoals—a proceeding which would almost certainly bring destruction.   In August, 1874, one did ground upon a bank of sand.   She was heavily laden with coal, and when the tide fell it swept the sand from under her bows, leaving their great weight unsupported.   The natural consequence was, that the vessel broke in two amidships, and became nearly a total loss.

Brunshausen, the port of Stade, on the opposite bank, is the next noticeable collection of houses after leaving Glückstadt astern.   Here is a little creek, off the mouth of which lies the anchorage where the

Hamburg-American screw steam liners coal and unload, their draught of water preventing their going higher up with a full cargo on board. They are fine, handsome, powerful vessels, of about three thousand tons burden, brig-rigged, and capable of sailing well upon an emergency, without the assistance of their engines.

The ill-fated "Schiller," wrecked last year on the Scilly Rocks, with the loss of some hundred lives, was one of this line, and it was either she or the "Goethe," alongside whose colossal hull our little white-winged bird of passage glided, for a few moments almost becalmed. Anchored near her lay two North-country "Geordie" brigs, displaying in bold letters on their squat sterns, the sylph-like appellations "John," and "Nicholas Smirk." Wonderful old tubs of a bygone age they were, looking as if they could hardly go a mile to windward in a month. And dirty! Fortunately coal does not smell, but guano does, and that happened to be the highly scented cargo of the "Cuba" barque, a hundred yards further up the river.

For these reasons the odoriferous neighbourhood of Brunshausen, on this particular day could not be recommended as an anchorage for yachts, although at other times it may be chosen. There is an inn close to the bank, a good landing place, and no scarcity of provisions, as we proved on the occasion of a subsequent visit.

Off Twielenfleth the breeze considerably augmented in force, and came abeam, giving us a capital chance to try the stability of the Widgeon. All the sheets were hauled in flat, and we held on with the big topsail aloft, while a strong gust blew over the land. Low bowed the lofty canvas, much to our pilot's consternation ; plank after plank of the lee deck disappeared under water, till the foam swirled about the coaming of the cockpit. Thus far would our beauty bend, and no further ; clearly want of power to carry canvas was not one of her failings. Thode looked immensely relieved when the sheets were slacked away, and she resumed a comparatively upright position. He was accustomed only to the "Fischerewers"* of the Elbe, which must inevitably capsize at an angle such as the Widgeon could quite safely incline to.

These "ewers" are the most curious craft imaginable, sharp at both ends, ketch-rigged, with masts raking different ways, gaily varnished hulls, and decked with bright coloured streamers flying from their tapering mast-heads. But the oddest part of them is under water. Instead of a keel, they have a long flat-bottomed canoe-shaped box, many

* Pronounced "ayvers."

feet wide, amidships, and diminishing towards either end. Hulls of no very unusual shape, as far, at least, as the waterline, are constructed on the top of these boxes, which contain the fish wells and a few stones acting as ballast. Of course they sit upright when they ground. These craft measure from twenty to forty tons, and seem equal in speed to average coasters of their dimensions. The Elbe was alive with their quaint forms, when we passed the Schulau light-vessel, at five minutes to one.

At this point there is a change in the character of the river banks. From the spot where the red roofs and copper green spire of a little town called Wedel, nestle among trees upon the left shore, bright sandy cliffs, overgrown with vegetation, rise higher and higher from a clean pebbly beach. The cliffs are presently succeeded by wooded slopes, dotted with picturesque villas, some very large, and of a castellated roccoco style of architecture. Blankenese, the watering place of Hamburg, is a pretty spot which reminded me strongly of the Isle of Wight coast near East Cowes; but the river is obstructed with shoals in its vicinity. One great nuisance thoroughly deserves the opprobrious name of Schwein Sand, for the obstinacy with which it resists the persevering efforts of a monster dredger to deepen the channel which flows by it. The current rushes through this narrow passage with such impetuosity that it is impossible to beat against it; nevertheless the water is hardly a fathom deep at low spring ebbs.

Hurried on the strong tide past this objectionable sand, with which we were afterwards to make a closer acquaintance, Neustedten was reached at five minutes to two in the afternoon, and a dropping wind carried us leisurely on past tiers of tangled shipping, off Altona,* within view of the great free city. Hamburg has a grand appearance from the crowded Elbe. Shrouded like London, in a filmy mist, the many-storied busy warehouses, the hazy forest of masts, and the old grassy fortification mounds, form an imposing picture, which gains an additional character of its own, from the three majestic spires, which overlook all, from seemingly unattainable heights in the deep blue sky above.

But on this occasion we had little time to admire, being fully occupied in trying to discover a berth for the Widgeon, behind some of the countless rows of warping piles, which fringe the river side. Every now and then, too, in a cloud of smoke, some little steam tug would bear down upon us with a helpless sailing-ship in tow, and we had to hurry out of the

---

* Pronounced Altŏna, the penultimate short. The Hamburgers derive the name from the Platt Deutsch, " All to na," "all too near," *i.e.*, for the benefit of their trade.

way to escape collision, which could have but one
result for us. Finding, after all, no safe resting-
place at Hamburg, we were obliged to sail back
half-a-mile, and put up with a corner behind the
steam-boat pier at Altona, where the Widgeon could
just squeeze herself into company with two or three
of her little German sisters. A landing-place lay at
the quay conveniently near, and we were also close
to Sauerland's ship-chandlery store, where yachting
requisites of every needful kind are to be procured.
It was not quite three o'clock when our pleasant sail
came to an end, after making good about forty miles,
in a little more than six hours and a half.

A few minutes afterwards we were all ashore, and,
hailing a cab, drove off post haste to Wiezel's hotel,
just outside the ramparts of Hamburg, in eager
pursuit of dinner. Then followed an adjournment to
one of the open-air concert gardens, where the night
closed in to the strains of Teuton composers. When
we got back to Wiezel's, the fact was painfully forced
upon our notice, that German music is incomparably
superior to German beds.

CHAPTER XXV.

HAMBURG.

The Alster—Uhlenhorst—The rowing club—Aspect of the town—
Conflagration of 1842—"Fleths"—Jacobi-Kirche—The Elb-
höhe—Altona—"Vierlanderins"—A break-up—Projected cruise
to the Baltic.

TWO bright warm days were pleasantly spent in
wandering about the intricate old streets and bustling
quays of Hamburg. Whenever we grew tired of
picturesque antiquity, our usual resort was the cool
Alster lake, bordered with modern villas and gardens,
and, on the town side, by a row of shops not inferior
to those of Regent Street.

The Alster is a small river, which has been confined
by means of a dam, and forms a sheet of water of
considerable extent, spreading into the heart of the
city, and adding much to its beauty. Little steamers
are continually flitting about from landing-place to
landing-place upon its banks. On board of these we
paid more than one visit to Uhlenhorst, a pretty spot,
where there is a concert garden, and the boat-house
of the principal rowing club.

Here, in the evenings, the water is to be seen alive

with racing boats of the lightest and latest fashion,
practising for matches. In the summer an amateur
regatta is held every year. The principal prize is
generally a large silver cup, for fours, which has been
won at least once by a Tyne crew. There are also
sculling races and matches for six-oared gigs. The
Hamburg oarsmen are always glad to welcome
English crews (although the German clubs can make
up good contests among themselves), and considering
the facilities for coming over from the Thames, it is a
wonder that more do not respond to their invitations.
Boats are carried at very low rates by the steam-
packets, which are only two days upon the voyage,
so that a week would suffice for the whole trip.

Most of the leaders of Hamburg society have
houses on the borders of the Alster. All are more
or less closely engaged in commerce, which cannot be
left to take care of itself, and so they live as near to
the city as is compatible with the enjoyment of quiet
and fresh air. The merchants generally speak our
language very well, and are no strangers to English
manners and customs. Ancient maritime and commercial relations have drawn London into closer
intimacy with Hamburg than with most other
continental cities, and an Englishman feels quite at
home there. The streets have a busy aspect not
common abroad, and as for the Exchange, it is a

sight to see in the afternoons, when its wide floor is literally hidden by thousands of brokers and their clients.

We did not visit the interiors of the churches, for the simple reason that they are not old enough to contain anything of much interest. The museums also exhibit few objects worthy of notice. Probably many curious relics of antiquity were destroyed, or stolen away, in the confusion which followed in the train of the great fire of the fifth of May, 1842, lasting for three whole days.

This conflagration involved in utter ruin nearly one-fourth of the central portion of the city, and although its effects have been thoroughly repaired, they are none the less obvious to this day, owing to the re-markable contrast between the ancient and modern buildings. The former are generally very tall, seldom of less elevation than five or six stories. Every stage projects outwards, hanging over the next below. High-pitched roofs and pointed gables are the rule, and the fronts are pierced from top to bottom with rows of little square windows. Much wood is used in the construction of these dwellings, and as may be readily imagined, they will burn like dry tinder.

Even at Amsterdam, the old burgher mansions are not so quaint as these, and the canals of the Dutch capital are not so darkly overhung with picturesque

A "FLETH" IN HAMBURG—THE JACOBI-KIRCHE.

warehouses as the "fleths"* which answer to them in
Hamburg. The still, black water of these havens for
barges reflects the queerest of tumbledown erections
of unknown age, clad in that sombre 'look which
pervades so many German things, one knows not how
or why. Here and there, out of seldom visited nooks,
the most beautiful artistic subjects are to be espied—
chance compositions with hardly a line or a light
astray from its proper place. One of them is here
sketched from a little photograph. The tower in the
distance is that of the Jacobi-Kirche.

I collected many other delicate sun-pictures in the
course of my peregrinations ; but the best are far too
elaborate for reproduction by the wood engraver.
One represents the view from the Elb-höhe, or Stint-
fang, as it is often called, a steep natural mound over-
looking the Elbe, and the suburb of S. Pauli at its
foot. In the foreground the most salient objects are
the vessels moored in tiers in the Niederhafen. The
spectator stands at a higher level than their topmasts,
and looks down upon the long seamy decks a hundred
feet below, whence, carrying the eye upwards, a perfect maze of masts and serried yards confuses the
sight.

* "Fleth" is the same word as "Fleet" in the names of many
English places, as Purfleet, Shalfleet, Fleet-ditch, and has the same
meaning as "canal."

The Elb-höhe wears on its crest a battery of cannon, but not for purposes of war, the moats and ramparts having been turned into a peaceful park. The guns are only fired when warnings have been telegraphed from Cuxhaven, at the mouth of the river, to the effect that a gale is driving the sea in, and a high tide may be looked for. Then, at the sound of their thundering signal, all along the bankside habitations, wretched people may be seen emerging from the cellars where they live, to secure themselves and their squalid property from an inundation of liquid mud.

Wiezel's hotel, where we were stopping, is built upon another hill, near the Elb-höhe, and is closer to Altona, where the yacht was moored, than any other, which was the main reason for going there. Altona, late a Danish town, is in all but name part of Hamburg, and with S. Pauli, constitutes a parallel to the London East-end.

It is full of music halls, clothing stores, cheap photographers, and curiosity shops, where ancient mariners bring for sale manufactured mermaids and other strange productions of foreign countries. There is little of interest in the town, but we had to pass through it more than once to reach the Widgeon, which had become quite an attraction to the yachting men of Hamburg, a few of whom, as Hescroff told me, had already paid visits of inspection during our absence. From another source, I was informed that a regatta was to take place very shortly, and was asked, at the same time, if it was true that I had come with the intention of racing. This took me rather by surprise, as I had no idea that any interest was taken in yachting at Hamburg. However, on making enquiries, we learnt that the approaching regatta was that of the North German Yacht Club, and was fixed for the second of August.

Fortunately Dr. Wolff was able to introduce me to Herr Wentzel, one of the members, and through him I made a request to be allowed to sail, which the Committee courteously acceded to. The Widgeon was at once put under sailing orders for Brunsbüttel, where I hoped to have time enough to put her ashore, to get the accumulations of sea-weed removed from her keel and garboard strakes, and to land a large quantity of heavy cruising stores, which overloaded her for racing.

On our way back to Hamburg we passed a crowded market of vegetables and fruit. Here sat a few of the curiously-dressed women called "Vierländerins," from the village where they live and pursue their hereditary calling — greengrocery. Their costume consists of a short frock and sleeveless jacket, the latter richly embroidered and studded with buttons of mother-of-pearl, or of silver filagree, in the case of the fashionable flower girls. They wear slippers and white stockings, and have light loose sleeves attached under the armholes of their gaudy bodice. The queerest institution of all is the head gear, which is a round straw hat, nearly two feet in diameter, and shaped like a circular rampart enclosing a central mound. In this mound the head is inserted. To put the finishing touch to the grotesque concern, an immense bow of shiny black tarpaulin is fastened on behind. Each loop stands out stiffly on either side, beyond the brim of the hat, and the free ends reach down the back to the waist, in loving company with two long plaits of the Vierländerin's own brown hair.

Not very long ago an English clergyman, who was living in the neighbourhood, created some excitement among these girls by purchasing all their silver buttons he could lay hands on. No one knows what he did with them afterwards, and he gave no reasons for his eccentricity.

Children duly appreciate and admire the Vierländerin habiliments. One or two shops have their windows full of nothing else than dolls of every shape and size, dressed up in this picturesque manner.

The time now came for the Passenger, whom we had found at the Hôtel de l'Europe, to leave us, after nearly a month's pleasant companionship. Our farewells were made at a dinner the evening before the Widgeon was to start for Brunsbüttel. No one had more thoroughly enjoyed our adventures than the Passenger ; and ever since his accession to our party at Brussels he had disproved in the happiest manner the trite old proverb, "two's company and three's none." Some engagement or other necessitated his presence in London, and the unwilling break up of our little party.

We began to feel quite sentimental. The novelty and freshness of our cruise had not even begun to wear off, and we could have continued it for months with pleasure, but the season of the year already caused me to think about preparations for the return voyage, although we had not seen a tithe of the interesting country within reach. The army of tourists loses much by not invading North Germany and Holland. Unvisited antique places like Emden, Groningen, Lübeck, and Bremen, must, at any rate, be well worth seeing once, and then for a yachting man, there could be nothing more delightful than a summer cruise among the countless islands of the Baltic. In Hamburg we heard enthusiastic descriptions of the game to be shot there, the green wooded slopes down to the water's edge, the beauty of Kiel harbour, and of Copenhagen. The Eider ship-canal, crossing the north of Holstein, would have given us a short cut in, and for a time I had serious thoughts of laying the Widgeon up at Brunsbüttel for the winter, on the chance of being able to sail her into the Baltic the next year.

After discussing this and a crowd of other schemes, we finally separated ; the Passenger to go on board the London steamer, and the Mate, my brother and I to take up our quarters in the Widgeon for the night, so as to be ready for an early start next day.

CHAPTER XXVI.

HAMBURG TO BRUNSBÜTTEL AND BACK.

Ashore on the Schwein sand—Anchorage at Brunshausen—The brig
"Superb," of Poole—Story of a special correspondent—Brunsbüttel—A squall of wind—Shifting ballast—The Widgeon's
"stowaway"—The North German Yacht Club Regatta.

ON Thursday morning, July 30, the Widgeon was
off by 7 a.m., beating down the river against a very
light wind, without the assistance of a pilot. In
about an hour's time Blankenese was reached, and in
the haze, mistaking a boat at anchor for one of the
buoys, we ran her helplessly on that Schwein Sand
for which no epithet can be too invidious. Before
long, the quickly-ebbing tide rendered our situation
the exact counterpart of the sandbank adventure in
Poole harbour, six weeks earlier. However, as the
weather was fine, bright, and warm, we were not much
discomposed, and sat down calmly to wait and smoke
and sketch.

At noon the Widgeon was high and dry, but at one
o'clock she floated, the flood having risen four feet in
less than fifteen minutes. In the channel, directly
she was under way again, she was met by so fierce a

K

current running up with the wind, that by half-past two, with incessant tacking, her progress was less than a third of a mile. Nearing the gut, where the dredging machine was at work, it became absolutely impossible to make any way, although the Widgeon was a close-winded craft in a breeze and smooth water. So with much reluctance we anchored, close to the shore, and remained there until 5.45 p.m., when the tide began to slacken. Availing ourselves of this opportunity, we started again at once, passed Schulau light-vessel at 6.30 p.m., and anchored for the night off Brunshausen, where, fortunately for us, the guano-laden barque was riding no longer.

My brother and the Mate pulled ashore in the Waterbaby, in search of fresh milk, eggs, bread, and meat, which they soon found at an inn, where the landlady at first took them for Frenchmen, but became very friendly when she was convinced they were English. The opportunity of giving in change one of Queen Victoria's florins, which had lain useless in her till for some time, no doubt considerably relieved her mind.

After a dull night, the Widgeon was under canvas again at seven o'clock, wind light, a point before the beam. Off a little creek in the mud flats, named Vischhafen, we spoke the "Superb," an old brig, of Poole, bound for Newfoundland, but in the first

instance for Hamburg. Two of her seamen afterwards formed part of our crew at the regatta.

The steep green dykes along the sides of the river
look just like earthwork fortifications. There is a
good story at the expense of the special correspondent of a London paper, who came down at the
commencement of the Franco-German war, to inspect
the military preparations on the Elbe. Some officers
at Cuxhaven invited him to their mess, where a good
many healths were drunk, and a surprising amount of
information was volunteered, which the too-confiding
correspondent duly noted down. After lunch a
steamer was in waiting to convey him up the river,
always with an attentive officer at his elbow. The
correspondent could hardly write fast enough. " So
many thousand men here ; so many guns there : not
common guns, mind you, but Krupp guns, which
carry *seven* miles !!! " Then, in avoiding the shoals,
no longer indicated by their buoys, nothing could
appear more natural to a mind innocent of marine
affairs, than the pious fiction that the steamer was
trying to escape from some lurking torpedo. Many
other tricks were played upon him, and the result was
an article which is credited with having thoroughly
scared the French fleet !

As a matter of fact, there was not a torpedo in the
river, scarcely any of the batteries were armed, and

the country was almost denuded of troops! So ingeniously had the government gone to work, however, that until all was over, many of the German actors on the scene were as fully taken in as the unlucky correspondent, and, although they saw no troops themselves, had not the faintest doubts of their being in force close by.

Brunsbüttel, and a long line of the adjacent coast, was defended by a handful of about twenty men. My friend, Herr Wentzel, was one of them, and he has assured me that he believed in the existence of an army in the vicinity until long after the fortunes of the war had become no longer doubtful. Of course he remained all the time at his post, and had no opportunities for verifying the facts.

To return to the Widgeon; she sailed into Brunsbüttel harbour about 10 a.m. The steamer "Ditmarsia" had grounded, on the ebb, just within the entrance, and the Widgeon also touched the mud, but scraped through it at a fine pace, barely six inches from the other vessel's side, all her crew busily occupied in fending off, with whatever came to hand. Finally she too ran to a standstill, but the tide soon rose and carried her to our usual berth.

The unavoidable sojourn on the Schwein sand had given an opportunity of scrubbing the garboards and keel, so after a short visit to the parsonage, whither

Dr. Wolff had arrived before us by land, we proceeded at once to the work of lightening. Our largest anchor, some spare cable, and a quantity of lesser gear, were deposited ashore (where we should have done well to have left half a ton of ballast besides), and the crosstrees, which had been bent at Amsterdam, were straightened by the blacksmith.

At 3. 29 p.m., the same afternoon, we sailed away with a very light breeze, booming out the large jib to windward. The wind fell nearly calm in the evening, and at last failed altogether, when we brought up for the night, a little above the Kraut Sand buoy, opposite Glückstadt.

Saturday morning found us very early under way. A violent squall overtook us off Schulau. It was very short and sharp, one gust and it was gone; but that one felt like a severe blow. Hescroff had seen it coming, and we had the mainsail half way down— "scandalized" is the correct word—but it gybed over when the weight of the wind came upon it, luckily without causing any damage. Rain followed, drenching our sails.

At Hamburg we received the "segel-statuten," or sailing directions of the yacht club for next day's regatta. They only departed from the usual English rules in allowing shifting ballast, and forbidding booming-out—two regulations of a decidedly retrograde character, for the first is very dangerous, and also leads to building unseaworthy craft, and the second is a restriction on seamanship. Most likely alterations have already been made in these respects, for the club is going ahead fast.

In overhauling the balloon jib this afternoon we discovered a "stowaway" on board, in the shape of a wretched little mouse, which had bitten a large hole in the sail.

The morning of the second of August, by eight o'clock, found the Widgeon in her place at the starting-point of the regatta. This was off the Köhlbrand, a creek which communicates with the Süder Elbe in the direction of Harburg. Two classes of yachts and two of fischer-ewers, were lying there at anchor, with sails down, waiting for the signal, a gun from the umpire's steamer "Energie." We had plenty of time to examine our especial antagonists, which were all yachts exceeding 28 Hamburg feet in length, and were thus enumerated on the programme :—

Yacht.	Owner.	Flag.
Laura . .	Herr Ad. Tietgens . .	White with blue ball.
Auguste .	Herr H. M. Kramer .	Blue with white ball.
Nautilus .	Herr Ferd. Kraefft . .	Red with white ball.
Anita F. .	Herr C. H. Fett . . .	White with yellow ball.
Schwalbe .	Herr P. Jörjan . . .	Yellow with white ball.
Widgeon .	Herr Chas. E. Robinson	Blue with red ball.
Welle . .	Herr H. Wentzel . .	Red with blue ball.

Except the Widgeon, all were centreboards, and the Welle was the only other not sloop-rigged.

The Laura and Auguste were two beautiful craft, spreading a great deal of canvas on long and lightsome spars. Though broader and shorter than the Widgeon, they were about the same tonnage, and carried a great deal more sail. The Schwalbe, Nautilus, and Anita F. were pretty little boats of from five to six tons measurement, but the Welle (Wave), belonging to Herr Wentzel, was a very handsome ketch of nearly thirty tons, against which the Widgeon of course had not the ghost of a chance of winning.

Presently the saloon steamer "Blankenese," formerly, under another name, a well-known habituée of the Thames, came down from Hamburg with a dense crowd of the yacht club members and their friends.

" Bang!" goes the preparatory gun from the Energie, and our crew are told off to their stations. Hescroff takes the helm, the two Poole seamen out of the Superb see to the headsails and anchor, I tend the mizen, while my brother and the Mate stand ready to hoist the mainsail. The wind is very light, and we are going to set everything. Quickly the seconds run out—five, four, three, two, one, and " bang!" goes the starting signal.

In a moment all the naked masts are clothed with swelling sails, the serried line of hulls advances, and the race is fairly commenced. Our course lies right before us. It is about seven miles down the river on the ebb tide, round the Schulau light-ship, after which we shall have to anchor and wait for the flood. The wind is dead against us and it will be tack and tack the whole way. Our lower canvas has been all set in a trice, and the Poole men are busy hoisting the big topsail, so there is time to look at our antagonists.

The saucy little Laura skims along thirty yards on our weather; that looks ill, but we haven't done badly in getting off third, in spite of two extra sails to handle. Our German pilot, Mr. Bähr, is all smiles; and the Mate, who has had a tough minute's work with the mainsail, has already begun to overhaul the beer-barrel. The Welle seems to take matters very calmly; her mainsail is only half-set, and anchor not yet aboard.

"Flap! flap! flap!" Hallo! what's that? Why, our two square-rig marines have let go the topsail-tack, which is beating about like a whip to leeward. Never mind, we shall have it again when we tack; but in the meanwhile the Schwalbe steals up on our weather. "Ready about!" round we go, and sheet the refractory topsail home, a slight puff reaches it,

and we shoot up out of the Schwalbe's lee like a
rocket. Unluckily for us, that's the last effort of the
expiring breeze, and we have not half enough canvas.
Our topsail sets like a card, and the Widgeon looks
a trifle closer to the wind than any of her op-
ponents; but their light hulls are slipping faster
through the water. Presently, the Nautilus gives us
the go-by. Then the big Welle, just beginning to
wake up. We are still ahead of the Schwalbe and
Anita F., but the Schwein sand is once more to be
our ruin! The Widgeon's draught of water forces her
to give it a wide berth, and the centreboards can
fetch through, while we have to tack. However, at
the Schulau light-ship we are still fifth, and fondly
imagine we are going to astonish the yachts in front
with a smart piece of seamanship, in setting our balloon jib for the short reach back to the committee
steamer. The men from the Superb are entrusted
with the task, but oh for a Poole fisherman instead!
They have positively let the sheets fly away in the
air, and we have to shoot the Widgeon up in the
wind's eye to get them in; a manœuvre which is
rather complicated by some one, in the confusion,
hauling the mizen taut amidships, and getting her
in irons!

It is impossible not to use strong language! We
lose a minute in filling off again, and are now last.

The breeze freshens, however, and the balloon jib
does wonders. How uncomfortable they are beginning to look aboard the Schwalbe! We are within
ten yards of her again, when the Committee vessel
looms up ahead, and this part of the race is over.
Now we have to anchor and wait for the flood-tide,
to be started back to Hamburg. The times of the
two races will be added together to determine who
have won the prizes. So far the Laura is first,
with Auguste close upon her heels, Welle third,
Nautilus fourth, and then Anita F., Schwalbe, and
Widgeon. We are a thirsty party. After lunch
our four-gallon cask of "actien bier" is turned
upside down. The time draws on for the second
start. On board the Blankenese the band of the
17th Mecklenburg Dragoons has been playing all
the morning, almost without intermission, and now
both music and dancing have begun to flag.

At last the flood begins to run up, and the preparatory gun explodes with a loud report. A fresh
wind is whitening the water with foam ; we shall
have it on our starboard quarter, so a little ballast
up to windward will do no harm. In the meantime,
if the starting-gun is not fired soon, two or three
of our companions will be off and away up the river
in spite of all their anchors. "Bang!" there it
goes, and only just in time. Our crew are on their

mettle, for their previous shortcomings, and I never saw sails more smartly set. We rush past the Welle, with everything drawing, topsail included, almost before she is under way at all. Our balloon jib is pulling us along like a steam-tug. The Widgeon's full quarters throw up a tremendous wave astern, which keeps her pursuers at any rate out of her wake. Nevertheless, the big Welle, once fairly under canvas, makes nothing of going through her lee, and is evidently bound to be first boat in. Twenty yards ahead of us the Nautilus and Laura, double-reefed, and shipping bucketfuls of water, are having a very lively luffing match, the excitement of which to them is much enhanced by our being so very close at their heels. We cannot gain an inch upon them, although we are dropping the Schwalbe and Anita; but I see the Auguste's blue and white flag drawing nearer from the distance astern. She, unlucky boat, fouled her anchor in getting away, and lost a considerable time. As for the Widgeon, it soon becomes evident that her bolt has been shot at the start. The Auguste finally passes us, but at least we are not quite last this time. The Energie is rounded off Neumühlen, and we glide under the stern of the Blankenese, to show the Widgeon off to the crowd of interested spectators, who kindly give us a cheer. Now, then, who has won? It is our friend the Welle, two hours thirty-three minutes and eleven seconds over the course. This is her maiden victory, and the prize is a silver centrepiece. The Laura wins the second prize, barely four minutes behind her big sister; but she has only beaten the Auguste by thirty-three seconds.

The "Chin-chin," Herr W. Robertson, a very pretty boat, and the "Emilie," Herr J. Pfeiffer, vanquished the "Monsoon," "Typhoon" and "Pirat," and carried off well-won prizes in the second class of yachts; while schiffers J. Cikander and H. Ferse-mann steered the lucky winners among the fischer-ewers.

By six o'clock we were ashore again, and then the Mate, my brother, and I took our passage to Uhlen-borst, in one of the Alster screw-steamers, to dine with Herr Wentzel. The Hamburg yachtsmen have a happy way of making strangers feel at home, and we passed a delightful evening, to which I look back as one of the chief pleasures of our cruise. Since then, they have been so good as to elect me an honorary member of the North German Yacht Club, and now that I can fly its burgee, my wishes are all the livelier for its future success and prosperity, which are sure to be maintained under the presidency of Herr Wentzel.

CHAPTER XXVII.

THE ELBE TO LONDON. CONCLUSION.

Homeward-bound—Fresh breeze in the Elbe—Brunsbüttel harbour flooded—A council of war—Departure of the Mate—A waterspout —Sail to Hamburg—End of the cruise—The "Iris"—Last glimpse of the Widgeon—Gale at sea—London—Poole—Swanage— Conclusion.

ON Monday, the third of August, the Mate and I began to think seriously about cruising homeward. Between the Elbe outer light-ship and the very nearest part of the English east coast, four hundred miles of the restless German ocean intervened. If the wind were to prove adverse, which it most likely would, the voyage would be very long and harassing, even supposing autumn gales did not force us to turn back. Then there would be a difficulty in stowing provisions and fresh water, besides many minor inconveniences which collectively put a decided veto on such a scheme.

On the other hand, we did not particularly want to retrace our steps, one by one, over the precise track which had been followed on the outward cruise; but that objection was not altogether insuperable. In the end the proposition to go back through Holland again, varying our course according to the weather, was carried very unanimously. With great confidence we set about provisioning at once, and before evening a cargo of dainties had found its way on board the Widgeon as the result of our marketing. Hasty farewells were taken of Hamburg, without the slightest notion of revisiting it, at least that year; and the night was passed in the cabin of the yacht off Altona.

Next morning, a light puffy breeze wafted us along with much deliberation towards Brunsbüttel. At four in the afternoon, Schwarz-tonnen Sand was left astern, but a calm shortly afterwards forced us to anchor off Glückstadt, although not on the same side of the river. Night closed in, damp, cold, and disagreeable, with signs of wind, but our little wandering home was cheerful enough within. One spirit lamp fell to work at once to make our kettle simmer and boil, while the other was cooking a delicious curry. These and other household operations lasted until quite late at night.

At sunrise, on Wednesday, a strong cold wind was blowing straight up the river, but our anchorage being protected by a corner of the embankment, we did not see the necessity for more than a single reef at first. Past Freiburg, however, the increasing sea compelled us to heave-to, tie up another set of points, and shift to a smaller jib. It was lucky we did so, for on getting out of the dyke's lee, into the equivalent of " Sea Reach " in the Thames, we entered a long channel of broken water, open to the German ocean, up which the wind was blowing hard against a fierce tide. The waves were very short and high, and the breeze, though not quite so strong as that we encountered in the Solent on the twenty-fifth of June, kept our lee gunwale well swept with rushing white foam. The Widgeon behaved beautifully, although she did nip off the crest of one or two transparent combers, piled unfairly high and steep, in the squalls.

Within a mile or two of Brunsbüttel, we were passed by the steamer " Ditmarsia," pitching her forefoot out into the air with a vivacity which was evidently not shared by her passengers ; and about eleven o'clock we followed her into the harbour. An English collier schooner from Middlesboro' was unloading at our old berth, and so we had to seek a resting-place higher up.

All that afternoon the wind increased, until a heavy sea was running in the Elbe, and the flood-tide rose many feet higher than usual. The next day it blew very hard indeed, and an old brig outside was having a fine time of it, with two anchors down and a great scope of cable veered away. In spite of all, the other Ditmarsia (both steamers bore the same

name) was driven slowly down from Hamburg, under
a press of steam, but the bottom of her keel could be
seen right amidships, when she jumped from wave to
wave in a burst of spray and foam. Steadily the
tide kept on rising, until all the water-meadows at
the foot of the sea-defences were covered, the customs'
shed became an islet, and the path to the Widgeon's
anchorage lay three feet at least under water. In the
general flood the harbour channel was quite obliterated, and the lofty slopes of the dyke, washed by the
turbid river more than halfway up their sides, began
to appear quite insignificant. Great excitement prevailed among the low-lying habitations, already in-
vaded by the water, in the midst of which a cart and
several wooden articles of different kinds, might be
seen careering about at the will of the waves. Fortunately but little damage was done, for on the 7th
(Friday), the weather, although still unsettled, began
to improve, the first signs of which were the grounding of the errant cart, and the re-appearance of the
footpaths by the harbour.

During all this week the Widgeon's crew were in
far roomier and more comfortable quarters, at the
parsonage, than they had been used to for many a day.
Time slipped pleasantly by, there was always something to be done; but meanwhile the barometer continued low and the wind blew steadily from seaward,

rendering it fruitless to attempt a start for England. However, the lateness of the season made it imperative that some action should be taken, and so one morning the Mate and I held a council of war upon the subject.

It seemed quite clear that autumn weather had set in, and that consequently it was out of the question to attempt crossing the German ocean. As for going back the way we came, with great luck we might reach Flushing in a fortnight,—towards the end of August, about which time strong south-westerly winds usually blow up Channel. The two hundred miles from Flushing to Swanage might then, in all probability, take us a month to get over— with neither pleasure nor comfort. A third idea, which had been mooted before, was to lay up the Widgeon at Brunsbüttel or Hamburg for the winter, but the uncertainty whether we could come for her the next year, caused this also to be given up ; and the only course left, was to sell her in Hamburg for what she would fetch, which I finally resolved to do, but not without regret.

On Saturday, the Widgeon with her crew on board, was photographed by the local artist of Brunsbüttel. It was too windy to hoist the sails, and so the picture was not quite what it should have been, but still was good, considering the apparatus of the photographer, who combines with his art the more lucrative profession of dentistry. Early in the next week, the Mate and my brother left in the Ditmarsia for Hamburg, to take their passage thence to London. They had a strong headwind and heavy sea all the way out, which delayed the steamer several hours upon her way, and quite confirmed the idea that the sea-voyage was impracticable for the Widgeon in the autumn season.

After their departure, I spent one more very pleasant week at Brunsbüttel, and for the first time in my life witnessed a waterspout. This phenomenon cannot be so uncommon as is generally believed. For instance, one occurred off Bournemouth about four years ago, and another off Swanage last summer. The Brunsbüttel waterspout, however, was larger than usual, and certainly looked very threatening. It made its appearance one afternoon, as I was returning with Dr. Wolff from a country walk. We had noticed a dense black cloud like a thunderstorm, coming quickly up from the German Ocean against the wind, and were hastening indoors to escape a wetting, when we suddenly observed a great disturbance and rapid revolving motion in the darkest portion of the mass. The next moment a long pendulous appendage began to droop downwards from the cloud, rotating around its axis at a great pace. The Elbe, which lay half a mile off on the other side of the dyke, was not visible, but a responsive agitation must have been taking place among its waters, for when the descending column had reached half way to the earth, another similar one rose all on a sudden into the air, in the distance behind the trees of the church-yard. The junction was instantly complete, and the whole spout visibly thickened and darkened, coming on with accelerated speed, although the wind kept swaying it violently about. In less than five minutes it had sidled across the river, and burst when it reached the land not far from Brunsbüttel, after which the upper part sailed away inland among the clouds, fruitlessly forming and reforming, for want of water to complete its continuity from below. The next morning the catalogue of its exploits was unfolded. It had caused no little excitement among the superstitious, and had committed the definite mischief of completely gutting a house and swallowing up a large pond in the course of its wild career.

It was on Saturday, the 14th of August, that I bid a final farewell to Brunsbüttel and the many acquaintances I had made during my short stay. Such a strong wind blew astern, as we sailed out of the little haven at one o'clock, that we reached Glückstadt by half-past two, making short miles of it on the hot floodtide. Later in the afternoon the breeze almost died away, and after an uneventful voyage, we only turned into our old berth at Altona between seven and eight in the evening.

Thus ended the " Cruise of the Widgeon," for my further stay abroad was only rendered necessary by the formalities which had to be gone through in transferring the ownership of my vessel to three German friends, with whom I saw more of Hamburg in one pleasant day, than I should have done in a month, alone. I still continue to hear of the little Widgeon's exploits from time to time, for she is in the hands of good yachtsmen, and is not stinted of salt-water and sea breezes. However, if I run on in this strain, I shall get sentimental, "which is absurd," as Euclid, that *bête noir* of my Westminster days, so trippingly remarks upon every possible occasion.

On the evening of the 23rd I went with Hescroff on board the steamer " Iris," bound for London. Early the next morning she started down the river against a stiff breeze, and passed the Widgeon not far below Schulau. After two seasons' constant sailing, this was actually only the second time I had seen her under canvas, except from her own deck ! Ask any really enthusiastic " Corinthian " (=amateur, in yacht-ing parlance) whether he has ever seen his own yacht under way. He is sure to be surprised at the question : and the answer will be—well, yes, he has, but only

once, twice, or thrice, rarely oftener than that. A
true yachtsman can hardly bear to think of his craft
moving an inch without his hand upon the tiller. As
for me, I scarcely knew the Widgeon at first sight,
but the wave of a white handkerchief, which was our
preconcerted signal, soon told what she was, and
mine soon bid her good-bye from the steamer's
bridge.

Off Brunsbüttel the wind had much increased, and
beyond Cuxhaven it was blowing a regular gale, with
spindrift and a very heavy sea. One little sturgeon-
fisher was passed near the middle-lightship, scudding
with a tiny rag of a squaresail before the immense
waves, which completely concealed hull, sails and all
in the hollows between their toppling crests. I fancy
the man at the helm was having an anxious time. It
very forcibly occurred to me that the Widgeon was
better off in the Elbe than outside it, in such a storm
as this.

After sighting Heligoland, we passed a Dutch
schuyt, hove-to under one little three-cornered bit
of canvas, and taking the bad weather very comfortably. The Iris displayed splendid sea-going
qualities, neither rolling nor pitching to any great
extent; in fact, a steamer could hardly behave better,
but it was all lost upon the passengers. In the night
there was more wind and sea than ever, and the

engines kept racing when the screw pitched out of water,—a state of things not favourable to sleep. One or two seas came over the bows, and, as Hescroff told me, rather alarmed the tenants of the forecastle, amongst whom were several young South-Germans who had never seen open water before. Somehow or other they had all had the sense not to contract by a single payment beforehand for their meals during the voyage, although most of the other passengers had done so. The price charged did not appear to the occupants of the after cabin at all high, when they were calmly paying for their tickets upon dry land, but at sea they soon reversed that opinion. In the morning at breakfast, not three people appeared at the table besides the captain and pilot, for reasons which had nothing to do with the cookery, which was not at all bad. As for me, however, the steward cannot have made much out of my contract.

In fine weather the voyage to London takes about thirty-six hours, but on this occasion, although the wind and sea gradually abated during the second day, it was evening before we made the Suffolk coast, near Aldborough, and coasted along in smooth water under the lee of the land. The next morning early, after a passage much nearer forty-eight hours in length than thirty-six, the Iris brought up at last in the Thames, the tiresome customs examination was hurriedly gone through, and I got ashore with Hescroff just in time to catch the train to Poole, and proceed to Swanage by our old friend the Heather Bell.

The Widgeon's moorings looked rather blank for the rest of that season, without the Widgeon ; but the next summer her place was occupied by a not unworthy successor, which, under the burgee of the Isle of Purbeck Yacht Club, will, I hope, some day follow the lead of her elder sister into other foreign waters.

APPENDIX.

ITINERARY.

The following table of distances traversed from day to day, miles sailed, time occupied, and conditions of weather, may prove of some use to any yachtsman who proposes to repeat, in a similar craft, the voyage of the Widgeon. The home cruises before the start on June 22, as well as those in the Elbe after the first arrival at Hamburg, are omitted as unimportant.

Date.	From	To.	Distance traversed in Nautical Miles.	Distance sailed in Nautical Miles.	Time.	Weather.
June 22	Swanage	Cowes	27	28	4 h. 20 m.	Fine: light wind aft.
,, 23	Cowes	St. Helen's	10	11	2 h. 30 m.	Fine and light.
,, 24			...	...	...	Dirty: much wind.
,, 25	St. Helen's	Southampton	17	17	3 h. 40 m.	Half a gale and rain.
,, 26	Southampton	Hamble river	5	7	4 h. 45 m.	Dead calm.
,, 27	Hamble River	Bognor	24	37	14 h. 36 m.	Wind light, with calms.
,, 28	Bognor	Shoreham	16	25	5 h. 35 m.	Steady breeze.
,, 29, 30	Shoreham	Dover	63	65	13 h. 55 m.	Strong fair wind, adverse tide.
July 1	Dover	Calais	21½	33	11 h. 18 m.	Strong breeze.
,, 2	Calais	Ostend	44	45	5 h. 42 m.	Calms, light breeze.
,, ,,						Strong fair wind and tide.

	From	To				Remarks
„ 3, 4, 5	Ostend	Flushing	31	38	8 h. 30 m.	Fine.
„ 6			.	.	.	Calms and light wind.
„ 7	Flushing	Treveeren	10 (canal)	10	4 h. 35 m.	Fine.
„ 8	Treveeren	Overflakkee	25	30	17 h. 30 m.	Calms and light wind.
„ 9	Overflakkee	Rotterdam	30	33	9 h. 0 m.	Fine, light wind.
„ 10	Rotterdam	Tollhuis	25 (canal)	26	12 h. 0 m.	Fine.
„ 11	Tollhuis	Amsterdam	20 (canal)	20	6 h. 0 m.	Fine.
„ 12			.	.	.	Fine.
„ 13	Amsterdam	The Pampus	6 (canal)	6	10 h. 15 m.	Fine.
„ 14	The Pampus	Enkhuisen	24	51	11 h. 30 m.	Fine, light wind.
„ 15	Enkhuisen	Harlingen	30	45	10 h. 5 m.	Fine breeze.
„ 16			.	.	.	Fine.
„ 17	Harlingen	Leeuwarden	17 (canal)	17	7 h. 0 m.	Fine.
„ 18—20	Leeuwarden	Dokkum	13 (canal)	13	4 h. 0 m.	Fine.
„ 21	Dokkum	Dokkumer Siehl	8 (canal)	8	1 h. 30 m.	Strong breeze.
„ 22	Dokkumer Siehl	Ostmahorn	4	22	5 h. 30 m.	Light breeze, and thunder.
„ 23	Ostmahorn	Juist	36	40	11 h. 45 m.	Calms and thunder.
„ 24	Juist	Elbe outer light	55	60	24 h. 0 m.	Light wind and calms.
„ 25	Elbe outer light	Brunsbüttel	32	35	9 h. 0 m.	Fine and light.
„ 26	Brunsbüttel	Cuxhaven and back	30	34	6 h. 30 m.	Very fine.
„ 27	Brunsbüttel	Hamburg	39½	42	6 h. 35 m.	Fine breeze.
		Totals	664	798		

Thus, excluding from the above computation the three excursions from St. Helen's to Southampton, from Ostmahorn to Schiermonnik Oog, and from Brunsbüttel to Cuxhaven and back, the Widgeon sailed in round numbers seven hundred miles on the cruise from Swanage to Hamburg, the direct distance by her route being something less than six hundred. If the cruising about Swanage, Poole, and Bournemouth, in June, and the several trips up and down the Elbe in August, are added to the general total of miles sailed, the number will mount up to considerably over a thousand.

The unusually favourable character of the weather is clearly indicated by the small discrepancy between the number of miles traversed and the number actually sailed, especially when it is remembered that the difference would have been much less had we not often persisted in tacking with a light wind against a strong tide, in which predicament five or even ten miles may be frequently sailed, for one of direct progress made. The distances given as traversed in the canals cannot be depended upon as more than approximately correct, as the maps never delineate their windings with any approach to exactitude.

THE END.

BRADBURY, AGNEW, & CO., PRINTERS, WHITEFRIARS.

THOMAS CARLYLE'S WORKS.

LIBRARY EDITION COMPLETE.

Handsomely printed in 34 vols. demy 8vo, cloth.

SARTOR RESARTUS. The Life and Opinions of Herr Teufelsdrockh. With a Portrait, 7s. 6d.
THE FRENCH REVOLUTION: a History. 3 vols., each 9s.
LIFE OF FREDERICK SCHILLER AND EXAMINATION OF HIS WORKS. With Supplement of 1872, Portrait and Plates, 9s. The Supplement, *separately*, 2s.
CRITICAL AND MISCELLANEOUS ESSAYS. 6 vols., each 9s.
ON HEROES, HERO WORSHIP, AND THE HEROIC IN HISTORY. 7s. 6d.
PAST AND PRESENT. With a Portrait, 9s.
OLIVER CROMWELL'S LETTERS AND SPEECHES. With Portraits. 5 vols., each, 9s.
LATTER-DAY PAMPHLETS. 9s.
LIFE OF JOHN STERLING. With Portrait, 9s.
HISTORY OF FREDERICK THE SECOND. 10 vols., each 9s.
TRANSLATIONS FROM THE GERMAN. 3 vols., each 9s.
GENERAL INDEX TO THE LIBRARY EDITION. 8vo cloth, 6s.

CHEAP AND UNIFORM EDITION.

In 23 vols. crown 8vo, cloth.

THE FRENCH REVOLUTION: a History, 2 vols., 12s.
OLIVER CROMWELL'S LETTERS AND SPEECHES, with Elucidations, &c. 3 vols., 18s.
LIVES OF SCHILLER AND JOHN STERLING. 1 vol., 6s.
CRITICAL AND MISCELLANEOUS ESSAYS. 4 vols., £1 4s.
SARTOR RESARTUS AND LECTURES ON HEROES. 1 vol., 6s.
LATTER-DAY PAMPHLETS. 1 vol., 6s.

CHARTISM AND PAST AND PRESENT. 1 vol., 6s.
TRANSLATIONS FROM THE GERMAN OF MUSÆUS, TIECK, & RICHTER. 1 vol., 6s.
WILHELM MEISTER, by Göthe, a Translation. 2 vols. 12s.
HISTORY of FRIEDRICH the SECOND, called Frederick the Great. Vols. I. & II. containing Part I.—"Friedrich till his Accession." 14s.—Vols. III. and IV., containing Part II.—"The First Two Silesian Wars," 14s.—Vols. V., VI., VII., completing the Work, £1 1s.

PEOPLE'S EDITION.

In 37 vols. small crown 8vo. Price 2s. each volume, bound in cloth; or in sets of 37 vols. in 18, cloth gilt, for £3 14s.

SARTOR RESARTUS.
FRENCH REVOLUTION.
LIFE OF JOHN STERLING.
OLIVER CROMWELL'S LETTERS AND SPEECHES. 5 vols.
ON HEROES AND HERO WORSHIP.
PAST AND PRESENT.
CRITICAL AND MISCELLANEOUS ESSAYS. 7 vols.

LATTER-DAY PAMPHLETS.
LIFE OF SCHILLER.
FREDERICK THE GREAT. 10 vols.
WILHELM MEISTER. 3 vols.
TRANSLATIONS FROM MUSÆUS, TIECK, AND RICHTER. 2 vols.
GENERAL INDEX.

MR. CARLYLE'S NEW WORK.

EARLY KINGS OF NORWAY; also AN ESSAY ON THE PORTRAITS OF JOHN KNOX. Crown 8vo with Portrait Illustrations, 7s. 6d.

CHAPMAN AND HALL, 193, PICCADILLY.

CHARLES DICKENS'S WORKS.

THE ILLUSTRATED LIBRARY EDITION.

Complete in 30 monthly vols., demy 8vo, 10s. each.

THIS EDITION IS JUST COMPLETED.

LIBRARY EDITION.

In post 8vo, with the Original Illustrations, 30 vols. cloth, £12.

THE "CHARLES DICKENS" EDITION.

In crown 8vo, 21 vols. cloth, with Illustrations, £3 9s. 6d.

			£	s.	d.
PICKWICK PAPERS	With 8 Illustrations		0	3	6
MARTIN CHUZZLEWIT	With 8 "		0	3	6
DOMBEY AND SON	With 8 "		0	3	6
NICHOLAS NICKLEBY	With 8 "		0	3	6
DAVID COPPERFIELD	With 8 "		0	3	6
BLEAK HOUSE	With 8 "		0	3	6
LITTLE DORRIT	With 8 "		0	3	6
OUR MUTUAL FRIEND	With 8 "		0	3	6
BARNABY RUDGE	With 8 "		0	3	6
OLD CURIOSITY SHOP	With 8 "		0	3	6
A CHILD'S HISTORY OF ENGLAND	With 4 "		0	3	6
EDWIN DROOD *and* OTHER STORIES	With 8 "		0	3	6
CHRISTMAS STORIES FROM "HOUSE-HOLD WORDS"	With 8 "		0	3	6
TALE OF TWO CITIES	With 8 "		0	3	0
SKETCHES BY BOZ	With 8 "		0	3	0
AMERICAN NOTES *and* REPRINTED PIECES	With 8 "		0	3	0
CHRISTMAS BOOKS	With 8 "		0	3	0
OLIVER TWIST	With 8 "		0	3	0
GREAT EXPECTATIONS	With 8 "		0	3	0
HARD TIMES *and* PICTURES FROM ITALY	With 8 "		0	3	0
UNCOMMERCIAL TRAVELLER	With 4 "		0	3	0

HOUSEHOLD EDITION. In Crown 4to. Vols.

IN WEEKLY PENNY NUMBERS AND SIXPENNY MONTHLY PARTS.

EACH PENNY NUMBER CONTAINING TWO NEW ILLUSTRATIONS.

Twelve Volumes Completed.

OLIVER TWIST, with 28 Illustrations, cloth, 2s. 6d. ; paper, 1s. 6d.
MARTIN CHUZZLEWIT, with 59 Illustrations, cloth, 4s. ; paper, 3s.
DAVID COPPERFIELD, with 60 Illustrations and a Portrait, cloth, 4s. ; paper, 3s.
BLEAK HOUSE, with 61 Illustrations, cloth, 4s. ; paper, 3s.
LITTLE DORRIT, with 58 Illustrations, cloth, 4s. ; paper, 3s.
PICKWICK PAPERS, with 56 Illustrations, cloth, 4s. ; paper, 3s.
BARNABY RUDGE, with 46 Illustrations, cloth, 4s. : paper, 3s.
A TALE OF TWO CITIES, with 25 Illustrations, cloth, 2s. 6d. ; paper, 1s. 6d.
OUR MUTUAL FRIEND, with 58 Illustrations, cloth, 4s. ; paper, 3s
NICHOLAS NICKLEBY, with 59 Illustrations by F. BARNARD, sewed, 3s. : cloth, 4s.
GREAT EXPECTATIONS, with 26 Illustrations by F. A. FRASER, sewed, 1s. 9d. ; cloth, 2s. 6d.
THE OLD CURIOSITY SHOP, with 40 new Illustrations by CHARLES GREEN, crown 4to, cloth, 4s. ; sewed, 3s.

Messrs. CHAPMAN AND HALL trust that by this Edition they will be enabled to place the Works of the most popular British Author of the present day in the hands of all English readers.

CHAPMAN AND HALL, 193, PICCADILLY.

INDIA AND ITS NATIVE PRINCES: Travels in Central
India and in the Presidencies of Bombay and Bengal. Dedicated by express permission
to H.R.H. the Prince of Wales. By LOUIS RÓUSSELET. Edited by Lieutenant-Colonel
C. BUCKLE, and containing 316 Illustrations and 6 Maps. Super Royal 4to, cloth, price £3 3s.

ROME. By FRANCIS WEY. With an Introduction by W. W.
STORY. Containing 345 beautiful Illustrations. New Edition, revised and abridged.
Forming a magnificent volume, in Super Royal 4to, 42s.

THE EIGHTEENTH CENTURY: Its Institutions, Customs,
and Costumes. France 1700—1789. By PAUL LACROIX. Translated from the French by
C. B. PITMAN. Illustrated with 21 Chromo-lithographs and 351 Wood Engravings. Imperial 8vo, half morocco, price £2 2s.

MANNERS, CUSTOMS, AND DRESS DURING THE
MIDDLE AGES. By PAUL LACROIX. Illustrated with 15 Chromo-lithographic Prints,
and upwards of 400 Engravings on Wood. Royal 8vo, cloth gilt, leather back, 31s. 6d.

THE MILITARY AND RELIGIOUS LIFE IN THE
MIDDLE AGES, AND OF THE PERIOD OF THE RENAISSANCE. By PAUL
LACROIX. With 14 Chromo-lithographs and upwards of 400 Engravings on Wood. Imperial
8vo, half morocco, 31s. 6d.

THE ARTS OF THE MIDDLE AGES, AND THE PERIOD
OF THE RENAISSANCE. By PAUL LACROIX. With 19 Chromo-lithographs and over
400 Woodcuts. A New Edition, on large paper, Imperial 8vo, half morocco, 31s. 6d

THE HISTORY OF ENGLAND, FROM 1830 TO THE
RESIGNATION OF THE GLADSTONE MINISTRY. By the REV. W. NASSAU
MOLESWORTH, M.A. Carefully revised and carried up to March, 1874. A New Library
Edition. 3 vols., demy 8vo, 36s. A Cheap Edition in 3 vols., crown 8vo, carefully revised,
and carried up to March, 1874. Price 6s. each.

A HANDBOOK OF ARCHITECTURAL STYLES. Trans-
lated from the German of A. ROSENGARTEN. By W. COLLETT-SANDARS. With upwards
of 600 Illustrations. Large demy 8vo, 21s.

THE LIFE OF THE GREEKS AND ROMANS. From the
German of ERNST GUHL and W. KONER. Translated by Dr. HUEFFER. Demy 8vo, with
543 Woodcuts, price 21s.

CEYLON: being a General Description of the Island, Historical,
Physical, Statistical. Containing the most Recent Information, by an Officer, late of the
Ceylon Rifles. With Map, 2 vols., demy 8vo, 28s.

THE PHILIPPINE ISLANDS. By F. JAGOR. With numerous
Illustrations and a Map. Demy 8vo, 16s.

CHAPMAN AND HALL, 193, PICCADILLY.

CPSIA information can be obtained at www.ICGtesting.com
Printed in the USA
LVOW03s1724130215

426961LV00012B/387/P